AFRICAN AMERICANS
IN THE
NEW MILLENNIUM

This Book is Dedicated To
My Younger Kindred

and to
Betty June,
Florence B.,
Ralph G.,
Wiley J.,
and Carl C.

AFRICAN AMERICANS IN THE NEW MILLENNIUM

Blueprinting The Future

by
Erskine Peters
Author of *African Openings to the Tree of Life*

REGENT PRESS
Berkeley, California
1992

ACKNOWLEDGEMENTS

Thanks to Mazisi Kunene for permission to print the quotation from
ANTHEM OF THE DECADES: A ZULU EPIC.

Special thanks to Beverly Love Holt and Michael Leger
for assistance in proof-reading
and to Nancy Kegler for assistance with design and layout.

Manufactured in the United States of America

REGENT PRESS
6020-A Adeline
Oakland, Ca 94608

Whoever abandons his home still travels with his pain.
Our greatness forbids us to flee from adversity.
The secret of life lies in the errors we commit;
Those who fail are also those who can rise by their courage.

(From Mazisi Kunene, ANTHEM OF THE DECADES: A ZULU EPIC.
London: Heinemann Publishers, 1981, p. 28).

A
Consciousness
to Consciousness
Interview

with Erskine Peters

Q: Consciousness to consciousness, Mr. Peters, it's been about seven years now since you did the first edition of the spiritual guidebook which is now published under the title *African Openings to the Tree of Life*. Why have you agreed to do this interview?

A: Because it's a way of giving coherence to my thoughts about certain issues that a lot of us are thinking about as we move into the new millennium; it's one way of blueprinting the future.

Q: So, the new millennium, when does it begin?

A: It begins really when this present millennium, this last thousand-year period of the age of Pisces moves into decline as it is moving into decline now. But the new millennium really begins to move out of its gestation or pre-natal cycle and into its own birth somewhere after the year Two Thousand, plus a century or so later.

Q: So this is the gestation phase that we are in now as the Twentieth Century comes to a close?

A: Yes, we're in the phase in which we ought to be looking deeply into ourselves and thinking about the pre-natal care we should be giving to ourselves to nurture that within us which we want to bring to birth in the new millennium shortly after the year 2000.

Q: And what do you want to bring into birth?

A: A greater consciousness of the world self, a me that is a world self which knows who I am, works with what I am and tries to comprehend all of that from which I am derived. I want to know the lessons of that derivation for the creation of a world consciousness within myself, and to know the dynamics of where I am in space and time, and to be self-affirming through my cosmic identity more than through anything else. You know, as we move through life, we have to always be aware of what blueprints we're using to chart and be careful to channel the various aspects of our lives.

It's always important to take inventory of self periodically. So it is as we enter the new millennium we have to look at time, circumstance and history to see where the blueprints are working and where they are not working. Some people may think that they are not using a blueprint but actually they are. All behavior patterns are blueprints and since we are going to behave in one pattern or another, why not study and assess our patterns and create behavior patterns or blueprints which are going to bring the greatest long term benefits? What's the use of not knowing what blueprint you're operating by and letting yourself remain a constant victim to it? However, once you know your blueprint and begin to determine the flaws in it, you can begin to alter your consciousness and behavior patterns to produce effective change.

Q: So specifically, where does one begin?

A: One begins first with oneself and one's children to cultivate a broad-based spirituality which allows one to recognize and draw from all the great wisdom of the world. Thus I am preparing to be the Omni-American, to use a term used by Albert Murray in his book by that title. To really be an American is to be of plural cultural consciousness. Although I understand that I am a biological and cultural fragment of Africans, Europeans, and Native Americans, I have no problem with *wholeness* due to being made of fragments. That's because I perceive the axis of my being to be the human essence, not the ethnic or racial essence. Those first generations of my African ancestors, who experienced fragmentation and dispossession, were self-sacrificing and philosophical enough to frame a legacy for me (us) upon which we could establish and maintain a sense of wholeness and human integrity while under siege. If we're too foolish to use the sacrifices that they turned into a legacy of wisdom for sustaining our wholeness, a legacy passed on in the spirituals, the folktales, the blues, jazz, gospel, and all — then that's our fault! It's our fault if we opt for *nothingness* after all the torment and hell those earlier generations went through.

Q: Why can't you just be American?

A: Because the word "American" is so polluted. Because the public might confuse my identity with many pernicious, conservative, reactionary, and racist elements in the country who have sought to usurp that designation away from the people-nation unto themselves. So, the word "American" needs first to be cleaned up.

The crucial question of identity for everyone living in America who is truly interested in the continuance and improvement of this nation is "Am I working to institute a democracy or am I working to institute only myself as the democracy?" This is the true question of American patriotism. We've had enough and too much of the negative type. It is the type of essential destiny question raised so eloquently in Gwendolyn Brooks's marvelous but haunting poem "Negro Hero" about the nature of patriotism. That's one poem every American should read. It is an essential part of our national literature because that poem embodies our essential mandate or embodies what we might call one factor of the American imperative which is not to lose the historical opportunity to create a democratic nation. I imagine that there are a lot of people who already think that's been done, that a democratic nation has been created, and that kind of thinking is a major part of our tragedy. I mean people in this country don't know the difference between democracy and capitalism. That's tragic for us all, tragic for the mark we'll leave on human history.

Q: You say "one factor" of the American imperative. Are there others?

A: Yes, one other major factor is to change our view and interaction with the natural environment. We can't continue to let the capitalist mentality toward the environment determine our future. If we do, we won't have a future. But we do remember, of course, that the problems we are having with the natural environment and the problems we're having with the interference of racism in the evolution of the democratic nation are directly related. They stem from the same causal process, exploitation.

Q: So what are you for?

A: Democracy is what I'm for. I'm just against capitalist exploitation. You see, a lot of Americans really think they are living in a democracy but what they're really living in is a capitalist state which exploits democracy. Would the same number of people love America so much as they say they do if they didn't think they'd be allowed to make all the money they could in almost any way they could? That's the test of the democratic nation and of our democratic future.

Q: But how can I as a non-white lay claim to America when the white power holder does not want to include me in the power alliance?

A: You lay claim to America by being America and by living within the Omni-American consciousness. You incarnated to live this lifetime in America. So you have to transform your consciousness to live the life fully and truthfully. You incarnated here by cosmic design not so much by human design. The human beings who brought you here are just the vehicular and circumstantial factor. It doesn't matter who has the illusion of holding the power in this country. The fact is that this historical experiment in democracy, which is an attempt on the cosmic level for the evolution of general human consciousness, becomes non-existent without you.

That is, American democracy fails without you; it plunges into nothingness and takes its place in the cycle of human failures without you, the African descendent. Remember, decisions about you are not being made only in the realm of the human but also in the realm of the cosmic. That's why you have to beware of vengeance and other negative emotions because they blind you to your cosmic function. So what Ralph Ellison was saying in *Invisible Man* is profoundly true, you are the destiny of white Americans as well as of yourself. That's inescapable no matter which way the curtain falls. So the people with the illusion of power in this nation might as well acknowledge that and get on with the show. And in the same way what happened to the Native American is a pervasive factor in all our destiny. We cannot deny that we are beneficiaries of a horrible legacy and that no matter what deeds we may hold to "our" property, this American real estate, we will always be living in disputed territory.

Q: Can America become a better and greater nation?

A: Well, yes.

Q: How?

A: By looking at its pantheon of trail blazers for democracy, small and imperfect though that pantheon may be: Black Elk, Frederick Douglass, Lillian Smith, Sojourner Truth, Henry Adams, John Brown, John Hammond, A. Phillip Randolph, Maria Stewart, etc.

Q: How else?

A: By mastering the wherewithal to separate in our thinking "democracy" and "free enterprise" from capitalism. The forces of capitalism and democracy have a contradictory relationship. So in our "democratic" nation it is really the capitalists who nominate candidates for President, we just vote for their nominations. Our political arena is in awful condition. Look at who we have for final candidates in a country with all these millions of talented citizens!

Q: What about racial identity?

A: Well, again, I repeat, specifically, that I am an African-Indo-Euro American because I am both a biological and cultural fragment of Africans, of Native Americans (who entrusted their blood to my lineage) and of Europeans who imposed their blood upon my lineage or seduced me into it. And I'm not bothered by these fragments because first of all my soul-force, my inner-head, my spiritual intellect, defines the wholeness of my being. This defining is not done by my racial aspect.

My soul-force is the true guardian of my ontology, my state of being, and it is that, my soul force, not the power of the outer-head and other outer forces, which grounds me as a cosmic being. And you see, my cosmic essence is more important to me than any other essence. These issues of race and gender, while very immediate and very affecting, are matters or manifestations of cosmic circumstance and are indeed not fixed. Neither circumstance, race, nor gender is fixed for the soul, but these things are just passageways of experience for the growth and maturation of the soul.

The African American must never allow his/her status to be over-simplified by himself or anyone else. The African American lineage is complex in its totality, representing nearly every part of the earth in one person or another. So the African American is not and has never been simply an outsider in this country. That's just a rhetorical figure really which is used to call attention to specific aspects of our plight. In truth, the African American has been the outsider-insider, and still is that.

Our relationship with America, although it has had its restrictions, some of which have been very brutal, has been in many, many respects epistemologically, ontologically, and ethically very intimate. That is, the African American has historically been positioned in such a way as to be able to comment upon how the Euro-American thinks, exists, and behaves. The history of American democracy is in a large part such a commentary on such a state of being as ours.

The fact that I'm a fragment, a part of this and that doesn't plague me. Instead it gives me a sort of existential mandate from which I can draw great strength. It gives my life dynamism outside of fallible human definitions of humanity. It gives me the charge to create myself. Ultimately it stands for me as a metaphor of the wonderful interactive capabilities of creativity in the entire cosmos. I am happy to represent that. So if there is any truth in the idea that the human is the measure of all things, I can certainly see the make-up of my existence as one emblem of that great cosmic principle. That is why I reiterate that my existence is cosmic before it is terrestrial.

I've learned better than to take my definition from humankind! If these five hundred years in America have taught me nothing else, they've taught me that! One thing that Carter G. Woodson emphasized over half a century ago in *The Mis-Education of the Negro* was that African Americans must not wait for the general American population to tell them when they can plunge into life's various spheres. For the United States, he reminded us, is not the world, and we belong to the world and must pioneer ourselves into it.

Q: Where are we in our leadership?

A: We need to be careful about the savior complex when we think and talk about leadership. We need to re-define this savior complex, to critique it. The savior complex is something we inherited from Christianity which has a certain amount of negative value, especially when things get rough. You see, we need the plural; we need *saviors*. We need spiritual saviors, economic saviors, academic saviors, social saviors, medical saviors, scientific saviors and so on. There's something for everybody to do in the process of surviving, enduring, and transcending our condition. We need a lot of saviors; every community does.

Q: Would you say more about how this relates to Christianity?

A: Yes. You see when we inherited Christianity we didn't spend much time critiquing its form and its doctrines. One reason is because we had to spend so much time critiquing the European representation of Christianity. We mainly critiqued how its form and doctrines were perverted by slavery. That's where most of our energy was spent, so we haven't gotten to critiquing Christianity per se. And in Christianity there is the messianic complex which, when interpreted and taught superficially, shapes the thought of its followers to look for *one* savior or *the* savior. This gives people a tendency to look too much outside of themselves. And when *the* savior is not present in their world, they tend to become beleaguered, trapped in disillusionment, apathy, nonchalance, and despair. Thus, we should look forward to having and producing great leaders and to celebrating them, but the emphasis should always be on the plural! People have been pointing this out since the late sixties, but it just hasn't sunk in enough. And I submit that one reason for this is the superficial interpretation and teaching of Christianity.

Q: Why did you use the word "superficial" when you were talking about how Christianity is taught and interpreted?

A: Because the person we call Jesus Christ was a profound leader. But unfortunately Christianity has pretty much turned his message into a sort of cornflakes philosophy, a type of instant breakfast. Even his own transformation wasn't instant! It is crucial to remember that Jesus Christ taught more than the word *faith!* He taught faith in a spiritual system, a system which you have to use in order to express your faith. He wasn't just talking in the abstract, but rather in the practical about faith in the divine laws, laws which have to be unravelled and learned, and put into action. Thus, people have to be careful when they claim to be followers of Christ because they don't know all of what is involved; a lot aren't willing to do all of what is involved. Jesus of Nazareth became the Christ because he understood the laws of transformation, the laws of change. And something else is seriously wrong with the basic christian church with respect to gender. Have you noticed how absent the men are? Even though the church is supposedly headed by men, there are really few males in the churches, very few. When you see a lot of men in the church, you can believe that something brave is being done there.

Q: Can you say more?

A: Sure. Let's just look at the messianic concept further. Even Jesus Christ, while he might have spoken of himself as the son of God, did not say that he would perform the work singlehandedly. No, he appointed twelve other leaders. And these appointments were made according to his view of what people needed in order to carry out successfully the complex functions of life. So he appointed leaders who would symbolize this complex body of needs of the human being. To put it as Charles Fillmore put it, Peter was to represent faith, Andrew was to represent physical strength, James, son of Zebedee, was to represent discrimination and judgment, John was to represent love, Philip was to represent power rooted in the tongue, Bartholomew was to represent imagination, Thomas was to represent understanding, Matthew was to represent the will, James, son of Alphaeus was to represent order, Simon was to represent zeal, Thaddeus was to represent renunciation and elimination, and even Judas himself represented in some complex and paradoxical way, the generative and conserving function of life.

In Fillmore's words, all these aspects brought together form the twelve powers of the human being. They exist in all of us, and we have to understand and acknowledge them as the composites of the human if we are to fulfill ourselves, communally or individually. In fact, this is how Jesus of Nazareth became Jesus Christ. The christos figure is in essence the transforming figure. Jesus attained christhood because he mastered the art of the transformation of the twelve powers of the human in the highest ethical way. To have done the opposite would have been to have become satanic. Thus, to be Christ-like means a lot. It's a multi-faceted engagement. It means a lot of meditation, study, application and self-sacrifice. By the way, you'll notice that the emphasis in this present day televangelism and all has little to do with self-sacrifice.

We need to gather and study continuously and as much as possible the wisdom texts of ancient Africa including collections of proverbs, prayers, epics, fables, tales, *The Mwindo Epic, Indaba My Children, Anthem of the Decades, The Book of Coming Forth By Day* (commonly known as *The Book of the Dead*), and much of the other ancient thought. Then, we need to come along and study the texts we've inherited and created in the West or through the West. You see, we have a lot of preachers or exhorters but we have very few priests who plumb the texts they've inherited for the profound meanings, and we have fewer still who look for texts outside of those which have been handed down to them in order to get a greater degree of depth and spiritual enlightenment. So many of these preachers think that Christianity is the only spiritual light of the world, but I'm sorry to say it is not.

Another thing that happened in the inheritance of Christianity, too, was that we took up the bias of Roman Catholicism against Judaism. And we shouldn't have done that. That is, we shouldn't have overlooked the significance of Judaism in understanding how to interpret the Bible. Again, this neglect was a crucial mistake for black Americans because in following the interpretations handed down by the Catholics and the Protestants we missed out on the wealth of information which the Judaic interpretations in the Kabala and the Talmud have to tell us about the totality of being and existence, how to come into knowledge and understanding of this totality and how to use it to enhance all aspects of life: social, economic, scientific, political, religious and all. The Old Testament is not just a book of ethics; it is a book of knowledge. It is a book that explores and instructs through rituals and symbols the process of maturation into a life of fulfillment. But so much of our emphasis has been on hell and damnation when we've virtually already been living in hell and damnation.

In addition to the emphasis on the ethical we need to give more attention to the instruction about the spiritual laws for gaining and using knowledge which will help to pull us up out of this hell. But the bias against learning is so strong in our churches that I think we contribute unconsciously to our children's low success in school. But let me tell you that just because you are ethical does not mean that you are going to pass your chemistry class or your theology class. Jewish people are masters in so many fields because they draw upon a very rich and encompassing field of spirituality which is in its basic aspects a system which talks about all the laws which govern the nature of the universe and how to learn to decipher these laws. This positive attitude toward knowledge prepares one from the earliest age to understand that exploration is part of the eagerness of life. It was the attitude embodied in the wisdom that Moses brought out of Egypt. It is the heritage of Africa which was honed by our ancestors and which we would do well to study carefully.

It's not enough just to get emotionally involved with the preaching of the crucifixion. There's a much larger meaning at work in that episode which can really only be understood through the quest of the spiritual intellect. It takes a high level of knowledge of great laws of the universe in order to understand the particular ethical dilemma of victimization and sacrifice that took place on Golgotha. And so Jesus of Nazareth himself sought to instill in us a sense of wanting to know, a sense of inquiry and investigation and he urged us to use a formula which embodied that sense when he said "Ask and it shall be given, seek and ye shall find, knock and the door shall be opened." Right there is the formula for educational and all other success, but in our churches we preach all around it and all past it. Instead, to our detriment, we preach more about the miracles and mislead the expectations of our people while also distorting the true teaching of Jesus of Nazareth. For in performing miracles, Jesus was performing them out of knowledge, out of knowledge of the laws of how the universal energy operates and can be operated. That's why it is a travesty and sin for us to emphasize miracles without emphasizing the pursuit of knowledge. Because a miracle, anyway, is simply an occurrence whose manifestation we don't understand.

Jesus of Nazareth became the Christ because he had knowledge of the highest laws of transformation and knew how to use them ethically. You cannot separate ethics and knowledge. So unfortunately, we have had this one-sided emphasis for so long that we've built this simplistic, simple-minded, mis-leading thinking into the worldview and thinking of our people. But one thing we must remember: and that is just because we have been victimized does not mean that we will not perish! That's why we have to be careful about these cornflake religions. They'll mislead you to think that just because you are the victim that the world owes you something. But that's a more complex issue than what most folk know.

Q: So what do you think about the old often-asked question of Karl Marx and the idea of religion as an opiate of the masses?

A: Well, any ideology can be used as an opiate of the masses: capitalism, communism, christianity or whatever. These have been the three greatest opiates in our time. The important thing is that we critique our ideologies, and all of us do have ideologies. We're all held in bondage by the ideology of racism in America, for example, and white people as much or more than we are; for if white people weren't in bondage to that ideology, we, and America, wouldn't be in this predicament. Not enough of us, black or white, are struggling to get out of this bondage. There's still not enough moral courage in this country. We're not only Babylonians but also Philistines. But the problem is, of course, that whites see us as in bondage, so they think they are free.

In our adoption of Christian ideology we have also taken on a number of liabilities. As African Americans, we have developed a strongly interventionist worldview based on the notion and expectation that not only will "something" come and deliver us from our oppression but that in doing so it will put us on top! Now, what kind of truly christian worldview is that when the focus shifts from the need for justice to the need for dominance!

In emphasizing the expectation of "something" to come and deliver us, we often forget to emphasize for ourselves the very important and crucial factor of human agency as important for appreciating and adopting the interventionalist worldview of the intercession of a cosmic or spiritual force. That is, we often do not emphasize the necessity for our preparedness and training in all walks of life (economic, legal, social, political, artistic, vocational, etc.) in order that we may be used as agents in divine and cosmic interventions. Let me make again the point that just because we are oppressed does not mean that we are good or that we are innately ready to be agents for carrying out the good.

Q: So what is the function of religion?

A: To tell you the truth, I would prefer that we place greater emphasis on the word spirituality.

Q: And what might we teach ourselves and our children about spirituality?

A: We can teach foremost that the reward or gift of spirituality is resilience. That is, spirituality gives one the capacity to spring back, to transcend difficulties, and to maintain poise. We can teach that Time is not final. That life on earth is a phase in the long journey of the development of the soul, and that the earth is a place through which we are passing. We can teach that all religions are spiritual systems which have been created to help remedy the imperfections of humankind, and that one chooses a religion or spiritual system according to what one needs to work on for the growth of the soul. Thus, my children's needs may not be the same as mine in this life and for that reason I should try to teach them the importance of spirituality so that they can choose or develop the specific religion or religions that meet their needs.

We can teach through spiritual orientation that one learns what he or she needs to work on in his or her soul only by studying one's self. That the self grows by learning how to confront itself, by asking the right questions about itself in relation to where one finds oneself in space and time; that the answers to the questions asked about the growth of the soul will be revealed by properly shaping and asking the questions which one wants to have answered. We can teach mainly that spiritual systems are processes which help us to understand how all things in the cosmos are connected; that what we do to or for anyone or anything, we are also doing to ourselves.

Q: Well, what about leaders like Minister Louis Farrakan and Dr. Na'im Akbar?

A: Yes, these are two of the most "popular" "speakers" in these times. I'm not sure I want to say "leaders." They're especially popular on the college campuses, which is somewhat unfortunate because even the college students are responding to Farrakan the wrong way. They are carrying on about him as if he's got *the* word. These black college students, in their uncritical following of Farrakan, remind me of their white counterparts who say that Ronald Reagan is their hero. I evaluate the thinking skills of both groups of students as being on the same very mediocre level.

Q: Well, since you've critiqued Christianity so tenaciously, do you have anything to say about Islam, which these brothers represent, or about the rise of African traditional religions?

A: I hold the late Honourable Elijah Muhammad in considerable esteem because he not only had an economic theory but he put it to work on a grand scale and demonstrated what could be done. And it's really his demonstration of what could be done economically that I esteem. Some of the racial theory of Elijah Muhammad, though, was very unhealthy. For literal-minded people became more trapped in hating white people than in loving themselves. Hate can have a peculiarly destructive and corroding power as it operates within and restructures one's ontology or being. It's the same as what hate for black people does and did in a tremendous way to the psyche of white people, in the way it distorts the sense of oneself and reality.

So literal-minded people under the influence of Islam remind me a lot of the hard-nosed, recalcitrant, literal-minded, Protestant whites in the stories of Flannery O'Connor and William Faulkner. The mental processes in these people become so rigid that they are like zombies and are therefore frightening and dangerous. They possess horrendous wills. It's unfortunate to see black people lose their magnificent and hard-earned legacy of grace to that condition. And indeed it does become a condition in so many. So, Honourable Elijah Muhammad made great achievements, but now I do consider it a bit much to hear Muslims say that he was the fulfillment of Jesus, Moses, and Mohammed the Prophet. Now, I can read better than that, and all I can think is that the Muslims who say this must be talking to an audience which is not reading and studying the texts of these three great heroic figures for themselves. But maybe the followers are like this because they have sold themselves to the idea that they have a leader and don't therefore have to study for themselves. That's unfortunate because it means, among other things, that sincere investigation is not being encouraged or cultivated in the group. Thus, you'll find Minister Farrakan's speeches ladened with Qu'ranic platitudes, a sprinkle of this and a sprinkle of that, but not really much depth, keeping the audience in a literal-minded or superficial mode.

Q: So, what about Minister Farrakan himself?

A: Well, again it's a bit much to hear Muslims say that Farrakan is God's messenger on earth. Oh, Farrakan is smart now! He is a master of the seductive tongue of a certain type. He knows something about the art of rhetoric for sure, or let me say more specifically that he knows how to get to a certain audience to stimulate certain feelings, but I'm not sure he stimulates concrete work. That's because he uses a rhetoric that mesmerizes his audience — not unlike many black preachers, mind you. It's one thing to hold your audience's attention but it's another thing to mesmerize them. That makes people dysfunctional instead of functional. Moreover, he often mesmerizes them with outrageous historical distortions.

You know, sometimes information can be presented in such an outrageous form as to be stunning. It knocks you out of your proper thinking mode! For example, Farrakan says that Elijah Muhammad led the greatest organization of black people any place on the earth in the last fifty thousand years. Well, if you listen to that carefully, you can see deep down what he really thinks or knows about Africa. Such statements undermine the credence of the good points he may be trying to transmit. But you see, that's what happens when your primary goal, conscious or unconscious, is to try to stun your audience instead of trying to teach them. And it's unfortunate because when you are able to draw hundreds or thousands of people, it all becomes like an opportunity missed.

You see, too, Minister Farrakan is a great signifier; he's really tremendous at signifying. But while signifying can be used to execute teaching, it doesn't always work well as the fulfillment of teaching. That's because signifying by itself can easily become nothing more than castigation. Farrakan is a lot like the limited, fire and brimstone, hell and damnation black preacher, in truth. The difference is that he's just doing it mainly within the framework of Islam and the Qu'ran. A theology based on a pedagogy or instructive system of castigation won't work. Much of the history of the black preacher should have taught us that. That is, if they weren't castigating Pharaoh they were castigating the congregation. Needless to say, this mode leads to a sort of self-righteousness in the leader, or at least a projection of it. And that doesn't help the delivery in the long run.

Although Minister Farrakan feigns humility in his rhetoric, watch though that he uses a rhetoric of finger-pointing. Over and over, when talking about human limitations and weaknesses, he often uses the words *you* and *yours*, not *we* and *ours*. Listen especially to how he intones the word *fool* toward his audience. I'm not saying that some of our ways aren't foolish now, but this orientation can have the wasted psychological effect of lowering the self-esteem of your audi-

ence instead of raising it. I don't believe in flattery, now, but
the castigation method tangles the emotions of the audience, and when our emotions are tangled our energies are
tangled and we cannot function at our highest or optimal
capacity to create that better self and better reality which
Minister Farrakan is supposedly espousing. Part of his appeal
is in the fact that he not only has rhetorical skill but he
knows also how to seize upon the appealing topics and to
give his audience something of a good time.

Of course, we all have our weaknesses, but we need to
know what they are. And I'll just say that one weakness in
most of Farrakan's audience is that on some level they are
drawn to the momentum of Islam because Islam plays upon
the vengeance motif, and they really don't understand that
in a very naive way they are fantasizing about vengeance as a
vehicle to power and control, so out of that comes a very
naive concept of nationalism which is supposed to be ef-
fected in the United States. Naive because somewhere in
the corners of their minds they are even fantasizing an
Armageddon or armed struggle, though not owning one gun
factory or gun store!

Instead of thinking in terms of creating sophisticated
and shrewd modes of autonomy, which is what it's going to
take for our endurance and achievement here, Farrakan's
audience, by grafting onto the vengeance motif, is often
dreaming about a reversal of power roles. And of course,
reversal is not to be equated with systemic change, which is
really what is needed and what we all, in a global way, have
to be about. He's right to emphasize that one should always
be ready to read the time, to know the phase of the epoch in

which one is living and into which one is moving. But, of course, we have to always be careful to filter out his extraordinary exaggerations such as in his reference in his African American Summit speech to the Japanese as a *brown* people as if to force the suggestion that the Japanese claim some affinity with us! Let's not forget that the Japanese don't even want to be mixed with the Koreans, that they will hire detectives to search out genealogies to try to be sure that they don't intermarry with Koreans! I don't understand why Farrakan has to be so unnecessarily misleading.

Q: But wouldn't you say that since we are the only ones who have suffered the indignities of slavery and all . . . ?

A: Forgive me, but we must beware of seeing ourselves as the only ones who have suffered certain things unless what we are saying is absolutely true and well stated. Sure it is crucial to know just what we have suffered. That's important for the framing of a perspective, but it is also to our great advantage to study and know other people and classes and castes who have suffered similar things, if not in America, in other places so that we may learn something about improving our strategies for dealing with our own problems. But once a group or person falls into the psychological construct that they or he or she are the *only* ones ever to have held a particular predicament or situation, then psychologically they have automatically blocked off part of the reasoning power that will enable them to see the situation in a context that allows for flexibility of strategies for liberation and empowerment.

Certainly our situation has its unique features, but we must not over generalize them to the point where we lead ourselves into psychological debilitation. And that's often what happens when one overdoes the uniqueness of his or her suffering; that is, we participate in the intensification of our own alienation. Unfortunately, this rhetorical mode of overstating the uniqueness of our historical predicament is commonly used by some of our more popular leaders. Na'im Akbar's rhetoric often falls into this type categorization that we are the only people on the face of the earth plagued by this and plagued by that. Well that's a good way to add to people's bewilderment, I think, even though the intent may be to stimulate.

Sometimes Akbar has good ideas but he deals with them in his speeches quite simplistically in terms, for example, of the complex array of causes which are responsible for what he emphasizes as a loss of the sense of community in that large-scale movement and exploitation of Africans to and in America. And his generalizations of the history of the efforts of the black community are misleading — for instance, such distorted examples that after emancipation blacks were running wholesale back to their old slave masters, that you couldn't pry them away. Now these types of distortions don't help to put strength into the black community, what they really do at a deep level is to engender a greater degree of self-doubt than that by which the people may already be plagued. So as the poet says, "Speak truth to the people." Akbar's concept of the stages of community development is very good, however. He emphasizes starting with developing first autonomy over the self; then extending that to and within the family; then the community, and onto economic and political processes and defense and survival maintenance. He's actually best at this. But his distortions really have to be watched.

Q: So who do we follow?

A: I'm glad you asked the question and I'm glad you asked it in that way because the nature of the question says a lot about mental orientation, individual and collective. And the nature of the question also says a lot about destiny. What I have to say here goes back to point out the implications of the messianic complex we've inherited. We're trapped when we are looking and waiting for one person to follow. We do ourselves in by following that route. We should seize and put to use any thing that comes from anybody which is enlightening for us. It's a big trap to sit and wait on *the one* model philosophy. It is rare that some other person is going to be able to provide the absolute and perfect solution to life for someone else. The other person may be able to provide, however, a good, very good, or sometimes extraordinary basis for someone else to build on. But for the most part all it's going to be is a good basis or foundation. After that the individual has to make use of that philosophy and shape it toward the needs of his or her own destiny.

It is hoped that people will be enlightened and encouraged by what I'm saying here, for example, but they don't have to buy what I'm saying whole. They should take the ideas that motivate and leave what's of no interest. Everybody is different even though we may work collectively toward common goals. But if people are going to be optimally motivated, they are going to always have to take the initiative to be enlightened by others but beyond that to go ahead to assemble their own program of thought and action. It's like going into a store: even if you have the money, it's rare that you'd want to just buy everything.

A philosophy of life is something that you work with periodically. It's never perfect, even if you developed it yourself! It's only perfect perhaps for the moment and in its generality. But life is not constant, and so as life changes one's philosophy should be able to change too. That doesn't mean that you have to dump everything you've been living by; it only means that you adapt and re-adapt if necessary. So there's no excuse for each of us not to have established some kind of substantial philosophy of action for our well-being to live a healthy and decent life. Or at least there is no excuse for each of us not to be involved with assembling one. And if we are not involved in building one and in using what we have built, I would be willing to bet that the reason why not is because we are sitting and waiting for someone else to make one for us. And that's partly what I mean by the deep impact the christian messianic complex has made upon our minds. It can be very stagnating and humanly wasteful to do that. We don't need one leader, but good leaders who bring stimulation to our minds and actions.

And again there is no excuse for not having some kind of workable philosophy because there is plenty in the rich wisdom of the traditional African culture and as well in the experience of African Americans themselves. There are lots of excellent points in the African proverbs, epics, tales, and all. And at least since the 1820s in America, there are scores and scores of excellent points about how to deal with this new world experience in David Walker, Frederick Douglass, Maria Stewart, Harriet Jacobs, Martin Delany, W.E.B. DuBois, Ida B. Wells, Marcus Garvey, Elijah Muhammad, James Baldwin, Malcolm X, Martin Luther King, Shirley Chisholm, June Jordan, Tony Brown, Barbara Jordan, Richard Wright, Lenora Fulani and others, and even a few in Booker T. Washington. With this rich heritage, developed so often out of dire adversity, I think there is more reason for us to be impressed than depressed. We have all this in addition to wealth of materials which we can cull from other peoples and other cultures. Yet, I'll still say that while acknowledging what's perfect for me is not necessarily perfect for you, that nevertheless it ought be a habit among us that when we find something good, we ought to share it with at least one other person. That's important, sharing the good! Otherwise, what's the Cause?

Q: What about the educational arena?

A: The parents, foremost, have to be responsible for seeing that high standards are kept with regard to learning and to the conduct requisite for learning. Parents must always be involved in the learning process and with the educational institutions which their children attend. Parents must always remember that they hire teachers and appoint administrators and elect officials for one reason only and that is to set a high standard of learning in the schools to insure that their children will be able to nurture and develop their talents, so that they can enter adulthood and compete in the workplace for a worthwhile livelihood.

Anybody who blames the condition of the schools first on the teachers, officials, and administrators is misled. The agenda for what the schools are to do has to be set mainly by the parents and watched over by the parents. The teachers, administrators, and elected officials are only there to carry the agenda set by the parental community. So the parents have to keep surveillance of their children and over the learning institutions. That responsibility cannot be given over to anyone else.

The condition of the student body and of the school in general will always say a lot about the nature and level of parental concern. In schools, there is no real teacher accountability without parental accountability. And this is the case for the rich as well as for the poor. Teachers have to be watched no matter whether their students are rich or poor. Some teachers are inspired to teach and some are not. Like other types of workers, many teachers fall down on their jobs if there isn't someone they know they'll have to answer to. Teachers are workers whose products are supposed to be good students. The raw material they are supposed to be helping to shape or mould is *your* child, *your* grandchild, *my* niece, *my* nephew. So if what is being handled belongs to us, then we naturally ought to be the ones to show the most concern.

The irresponsible parent will have a hard time casting blame in another direction for his or her child's failures. A lot of children, for example, are kidnapped right in their own homes, right under their parents faces by such things as television. All parents should keep up, do something daily or weekly to check on their children's educational growth by keeping tabs on how well they can read or write. How many parents actually know this? They can use simple procedures to help keep tabs such as: asking them routinely to read the newspaper, textbooks, mail, advertising circulars, instruction booklets to the parent while the parent is preparing dinner, relaxing after getting in from work. They can be alert to see whether their child can write them a coherent note, add the shopping list, balance the checkbook, formulate and articulate their thoughts about a magazine article or newspaper editorial.

Anybody who cannot do these simple and basic things does not need children in this day and time. You have to ask yourself: What learning systems did you begin to inculcate into your child at birth (or before birth)? What value systems are you using to fortify your child before he or she leaves home each day? What did your child learn today? What did you learn from or about your child today? When was the last time you discussed your child's school offerings with another parent? When was the last time you discussed or thought about your child's success rate? When was the last time you worked with a group to improve your child's school? What do you do to reinforce your child's learning and success rate? This last question is very important. It is crucial to learning because it is through reinforcement that most learning actually takes place, not just in the introduction of the material in the classroom. That's why it is so important for parents to have their children discuss and summarize for them what they have done in each subject area each day. In addition, this exercise helps the student to prepare for classroom examinations and helps them to become comfortable with being quizzed or examined.

Training to be creative and competitive is vital. Our concern for preparation reveals the degree of our awareness about how to deal most effectively in the world in which we find ourselves. We all need skills, and skill is the mastery of energy, which is what we all are, *energy*. Many of our children are putting lots of their energies into excitement and other things that are short-lived. Pubescent boys and girls go along to school dressed for lounging instead of for working. You would think some of them were on their way to stand in somebody's store window for the day. They step along often without a book, pad, or pen. But they are supposed to be going to school! At the same time the states are taking money which could be going to improve schools and are using it to build prisons. Prisons for these same children allowed by their parents to skip along carelessly, children who will not have the skills to do anything much in the work place. We are helping prepare them for the prisons.

You know, I think one of the worse things we can have around is someone who is simply a pronouncer of doom. I mean the soothsayers who make it an occupation to go around giving statistics about how bad things are going to be. You know, like saying from one year to another that by a certain year seventy-percent all African American males are either going to be in jail or dead. It is definitely important for us to watch and study trends but we should not simply throw out statistics or poisons which are going to devastate or erode the morale of our people without also giving some formulas, solutions, initiatives or antidotes for counteracting or beginning to counteract the poison. For example, if drugs have been the number-one cause of black male deaths and incarceration in this country since the 1960s, we ought to be hitting that nail on the head by telling people not to tolerate any kind of drug activity in their homes or neighborhoods, to rally against it from the first indication that it's going on. We ought not to tell black people that by a decade or so the only type of jobs available for black people are going to be service jobs because of the increase in computer technology and all. To me, people who just do this are not leaders and are not deserving of much attention. The reason I say this is because if this is all they can say then they are denying rather than affirming the humanity and genius of black people.

Part of what it means to be human is to be able to look ahead at trouble and chaos and to devise ways of transcending that chaos. These soothsayers speak to black people as if they are some kind of fixed animal form, and I think this only lowers the morale in the community, especially among our youth. But if we speak to our people from a sense of affirmation of their genius, then what we will say instead is that the duty of parenting (which is to some extent all our duty) is to become obligated to seeing that our children have all the basic skills to deal with the new technology. Why use up our energy on dwelling on a proposed, fixed, negative future when we could be using that same energy to design and change that future? Just as computer technology is being invented, that means that some person is inventing it, and black, people, too, have inventive genius which can be cultivated to invent this technology. In the same way, black people have mechanical genius, and since these things are mechanical, the technocrats are always going to need someone to fix these machines. Black people have the native conceptual talent also which can be cultivated to design programming for these machines. And there are some black people who are presently doing these things. But they wouldn't be doing them if they had simply sat by and thought that the only future open to them was to work and serve hamburgers all their lives. We must always remember that the future is something that we can help create, and that the future will be largely determined by our present behavior patterns.

We have to take a de-mystifying approach to what could be perceived as a "magical technology" because anything that has a magical effect on you also has a certain amount of power over you. So we shouldn't mystify any technology or industry before our children or ourselves, we should instead de-mystify it. What I mean by that is that we should explore with our children how everything they use in their lives, from televisions, radios, computers, toys, robots, water faucets, refrigerators, on down to food and toilet paper comes into being or is made and constructed. Otherwise, if we don't have a sense of how these things are made or function then their makers and producers hold a subtle and forceful power over us because we have to depend on those others to make the things we need and desire. Basic information on these various subjects can be explored between

parent and child in the public library or the home encyclo-
pedia. This kind of exploration will not only raise the level
of knowledge and curiosity of the child, but will give her or
him a greater sense of confidence and self-reliance.

You see what I mean, if we don't know how to change
an automobile tire we have to call somebody else and that
person has therefore a certain amount of power over us. Just
think then about the power the person has who knows how
to make the tire! Then think about that in relation to
television, the refrigerator and such. We should teach ourselves and our children not to take for granted anything that
we use in our lives, not even the materials with which our
houses are built since the supply is exhaustible and that
always affects the quality of what we can afford.

**Q: Do you believe as some seem to hold, that white people
have an innate dislike for black people?**

A: No, I don't, even though there may be a lot who do.
Historically, we have just been a convenient vehicle for
their psychological displacements as well as, paradoxically,
for their economic success. Let us remember this. And this
relates to something that we must always remember if we are
to get a good grasp upon our reality. And that is that white
people did not come out of an historical reality in which
they feared black people. Probably nobody had treated them
with such great civility than the peoples of the continent of
Africa. But whites took advantage of that civility. (You
know how human beings do, take kindness for weakness.)

White Americans came out of a reality in which they feared *white* people, not black people. It's right there in their history books; no need to overlook that. Generation after generation it was one European tribal nation or nation-state against another. They try to ignore this when they broadcast with disdain and condescension the tribal wars among black or brown or yellow peoples. Go back to any European history book and read about the Hundred Years War, the Thirty Years War, the Twenty Years War, and all. You see, while white people are playing a dirty game with us, they are also playing a dangerous game with themselves, dangerous because self-delusion is eventually psychologically self-destructive. In all their monumental crimes, they are continually deluding themselves that they are the emblems of humanity. Well, that's a blind spot derived from vanity, and a mirror derived exclusively from the self cannot see everything; it will not allow you to see all the cars truly coming down the road. And that's their tragedy: they're in love with their blind spot! Of course, for us, that makes them dangerous, too.

That historically white people have been intensely afraid of white people is still a major determinant in their psychology. Deep down they know who have committed the greatest cruelties in the modern world upon others and upon themselves. And they know who is still most capable of doing so. They really ought to be down on their knees. Their history, not all of which they wrote down but enough of which they did, is an enormous horror for their conscious minds to bear, so they do what uncourageous human beings do, they displace the horror or avert themselves from the spectacle of their brains lest they see the projection of themselves. But white is supposed to be perfect, they have deluded and taught themselves. Thus, their own history is no reason for them to be on their knees. And this delusion has been institutionalized to be passed along to the generations, which creates a complex complicity between parent and child.

They, the whites, set a trap for a profound type of intrafamilial hate to be established within the family. They all aren't blind, but indeed one of the greatest anomalies in their delusion is that they who have created and used the most devastating mechanisms of destruction the earth has ever known have deluded themselves that they are not violent! When they hear the word violent they think about other people. It's enormously tragic, and I say this with compassion for our common humanity. But some among the white people are going to have to stand out from the fold and help their people to deal with their problems.

In addition, it must not be forgotten that white American psychology is informed historically by a sense of deprivation and inferiority in respect to their own European homeland, and this has crucially informed the way they have related and do relate to Africans whom their aristocratic relations formally placed at the bottom of the Great Chain of Being.

The white people came to America with an inferiority complex in relation to their own race, the white aristocracy of Europe who held the land and the power. They didn't come with a superiority complex. Much of their motivation in America has been to prove their worth in light of their kindred. So it is critically misleading to speak of or think of white people as dominated exclusively by a superiority complex. When we do that, that is, ignore the serious inferiority complex in their history, we make it difficult for ourselves to get a good handle and understanding on the origins of their psychology and problems. Go read what the upper classes of Europe had to say about the lower classes of Europe. I tell you it's the same language that the white Americans use about us. And this has gone on into the twentieth century: upper class whites developing biased tests and rigging the statistics to prove lower class whites as mentally inept and less capable than the upper classes.

And when you study white American cultural history, you see the other side at work.

That is, for years and years, white Americans spent lots of time trying to prove that they could create artistic and philosophical expression equal to that of their European relatives. But the Europeans kept writing back that they couldn't, saying that they could not create great art because America had no real foundation for "culture." And this debate went on and on, and still does to some degree in some of the areas like music, philosophy, visual art, and literature. It's all there in the literary documents of the nineteenth century especially. So you see what complications of psychology the Africans get caught up in, and these are determinants of how we were treated and still are treated. It's that old tragically fraudulent scheme of human impulse, that I'm so busy trying to prove *my* humanity (and by my oppressor's standards, dig that!) that in the process I feel compelled to deny you your humanity and fulfillment as a human being.

And of course, the great irony of it all is that this process leads actually and ultimately to the discrediting of one as distinctly human as opposed to animal.

You know, history has all kinds of ironies. And we must never fall victim to seeing circumstance as fixed. Only, the past, perhaps sometimes, is fixed. We don't want to forget that Anglo-Saxons were brought as slaves into Rome. And we certainly want to be aware of one of the greatest of Euro-American historical ironies, that although now the white woman is placed on a pedestal, that before the lynchings of black men in this country, a few hundred years before that it was this same white woman, now placed on the pedestal, who was burned at the stake by the thousands in Europe. But then, several centuries later black men were being lynched in her name. We must remember and consider this as a factor in the human psychology with which we are dealing. The paradoxes and ironies are important! You see what I mean by things not being permanently fixed!

Q: Do you think this coming generation is getting more impatient?

A: Well, that may be the nature of some of the anxiety we see today especially among black college students on predominantly white campuses. America can commit itself to solving so many problems within a certain period of time but refuses to give that kind of commitment to rooting out the psychological factors of its racism. And I think this is a major part of the collective intuition of young blacks today.

They are knowing that the dominant society sees them and their concerns as generally negligible. This is a real shock to a lot of these students who are trying to rise as much into the upper middle classes as they are trying to rise out of the strangle of racial oppression. When they leave the home nest and get into some of these college environments where they meet a significant group of whites, not all, who are really economically privileged and who may even take the privilege for granted or worse who are arrogant about their privileges, black students have to begin consciously or unconsciously to re-define who they thought they were.

This is not to say that the privileged classes are closed classes but when race is a factor privileged classes are significantly more closed. And the black students begin to feel this because made real now is an obstruction to upward mobility, which mobility they might have thought earlier was the raison d'etre of their existence. So they react in different ways, some in very liberating ways but others in demoralizing and stagnating ways which lead them to question their self-worth. The latter are demoralized, of course, because they have relied and obviously are still relying too much upon their oppressor's definition of self-worth and the good life. They won't come out of this stagnation until they create their own definitions and place their esteem in their own inner head rather than in the outer-head standards which are so often created to exploit them. But this group has to be careful, and not so much because of its racial oppression but because of its stifling, emerging middle-class position. That is, as Professor Sylvia Wynter of Stanford and others have pointed out, a yearning emerging middle-class will often lend itself to carrying out the greatest atrocities as a way of trying to purchase upward mobility. So in all of these cases, it is very important for these students to let themselves be nurtured by the noble spiritual legacy which their heroic African American ancestors have bequeathed to them. That is why the ancestors developed this legacy, because they knew there would be times when later generations, too, would need it.

Q: A lot of the most popular speakers today bring up the issues of the identity of the Ancient Egyptians and of melanin as a way of regaining the self-esteem of African Americans, what do you think of that?

A: Well, the reason, of course, that there is a dispute at all is because modern European identity has been shaped by the mental construction that anything approaching greatness must have been generated by white people. A lot of people get caught up in asking the question over and over of whether the Ancient Egyptians were black or white. I don't necessarily care for the motives people have in asking the question (as if the answer to this question is going to be the ultimate determinant of their identity and fate!), but let us say regarding this dispute about the "racial" identity of the Ancient Egyptians that they were not Anglo-Saxon! (You get my drift?) And let's say that if the Egyptians look like any group of people on the face of the earth, they look like African Americans because they encompass the total range of features of African Americans, that is, from glossy and dull ebony to pale white — the same range of complexions existing today in most African American extended families.

What I mean is that for virtually every physiognomy or visage you find of an Ancient Egyptian, you can find a corresponding one among African Americans. Among the Ancient Egyptian images that you've seen, have you seen the one of Osiris in Paris downstairs in the Louvre? Well, the venerable Osiris looks just like an enigmatic-face black man walking along any Alabama, Mississippi, or Georgia backroad! Suffice it to say that if most of the major Egyptian figures like King Tut, Akhenaten, Nefertiti (c1370 B.C.), the God Hapi (1318-1304 B.C.), Seti I (1318 B.C.), Imhotep, Nephthys, the Great Sphinx of Giza, Niai with his wife Isis, Rameses II and IV, etc., if any of these were born today to an American husband and wife or couple presuming themselves to be white, Anglo-Saxon white, there would be big trouble in the house. Had Anwar Sadat been born into a white American family, there would have been big trouble. So, if you want to know how to draw the line, that's how to draw the line! These white academicians will lay claim to the Egyptians in books and history, but many would not want to lay claim to them if these same figures were born into their families!

You see the Anglo-Saxon Americans have a shrewd way of garnering power by *allowing* certain cultural and ethnic groups like the Jewish and Italian and Spanish and Portuguese people, of allowing them to pass as Anglo-Saxon if they will support their policy of white racial hegemony, when certainly a high percentage of the people of these groups are not as white as some of my African American blood relatives are and have been. But you see, those desir-

ing the power of dominance will use anything at their disposal to gain and maintain dominance. And in the epoch of
the rise of the European, they found race at their disposal
and have been using it. In the same very fraudulent way,
white people will even press the issue by asking whether
Egypt is in Africa! And the answer is definitely yes: All of
Egypt is in Africa! But I tell you one thing, and this is
something they don't seem to notice, and that is that *none* of
England or Great Britain is *in* Europe. And only even a part
of Italy is *in* Europe if you really want to get technical. Some
of Spain even is closer to Africa than to the heart of Europe.

As to the issue of melanin: this is a very serious issue. It's
amazing how people can fall into using the same form of
thinking by which they claim to have been victimized. And
this is the case of the "melanites," as some of us have begun
to refer to those who are espousing black racial superiority
due to the very manifest presence of melanin in people of
African descent. I don't see any kind of beneficial logic in
trying to fight racism with racism, and it's very unfortunate
that so many of the young people are being turned on by this
fantasy. Even lots of college students. If this is the view you
espouse, then I say don't balk about white racism. If you
espouse such a way of thinking, then what you are saying is
that racism is fair-play. Moreover, with the great range of
pigmentations existing in African American families, even
in immediate families, it's very stupid, short-sighted, and
devisive to go around placing value on pigmentation.

I don't see how people can sit and hear these "melanites" talk and be so un-thinking in their response, so un-
thinking as not to consider all of the foreboding ramifica-

tions of what is being said. It's all negative in the way it's being espoused. All this espousal does is to send black people further off into a fantasy mode of thinking, like waiting to be delivered by some magical discovery, some easy solution. It's sad, real sad. Vengeance can make people so short-sighted. And these "melanites" often appear to be driven more by vengeance than by a true development of their own magnificence. The short-sightedness in some of the articles written by many and, for example, the author of *Journey of the Songyhai People*, is really amazing. Not only is *Journey of the Songyhai People* racist, but also tragically sexist in that the theory actually supports the white racist stereotype of black women as being naturally and innately seductive. This leads me to ask the question then of who raped whom during slavery. For according to the Songhai author, lip-size signalled sexual readiness, "the larger the size, the greater the readiness. The African females who developed this lip-size signal to the greatest extent were most avidly pursued." Well, this makes me think that rape of black women is something that's generally unavoidable. Now, that's sad. And people are swallowing it up! That's all I've got to say about the melanites!

Q: There are lots of discussions that take place in some of our communities about black male/female relationships. Although you've never been married, I know though that you've been on at least one or two such panels in the midwest and on the west coast. What has been your basic point about improving these relationships and how is this

now related to feminism?

A: Yea, we're all involved in male/female relationships whether we're married or not. Because if there are definitely real problems they probably don't start with marriage itself but are probably there long before the marriage takes place. And they have to be because what we are really talking about is something historical, cultural, and social, institutionalized in our modes and rituals of dictated and expected behavior.

In discussing black male-female relationships and the so-called failure of the black male which is so often alluded to by black women who want not just a husband but a black husband, we have to first of all be honest about how we are personally and collectively defining each gender. And I mean that unless we are honest in defining what we mean personally when we say man, black man, black woman, woman then we are just playing games with ourselves, fondling our own ego, talking to be talking. And talk is cheap.

One thing, too, that we need to do is focus on people who are really interested in having black to black relationships and leave the other folk alone since they are adults and haven't asked us for help. Specifically I mean we don't need to be giving our energy to relationships between black men and white women and vice-versa. But a lot of people get caught up in this and this to me points to some deeper psychological problems involving self-esteem and envy. Well, a person who is coming out of this motivation is probably not going to have a very healthy relationship with anybody.

If the woman is going to be a feminist, and by that I mean someone who claims her own autonomy and struggles persistently to help other women to claim that autonomy, all great in itself, then as a liberated woman she must never consider the male of the species as her protector. That's something that she'll have to let go, although many women who wish to claim to be feminists still want to see the male as ultimate protection. That's not going to work. Because when she does that she has compromised her achievement of autonomy and has probably only complicated the gender relationship because of what begins to happen when personalities are juggled by power.

Cross-signalling causes stress. This engenders frustration and the result, though sometimes delayed and latent, can be quite vicious and violent. All relationships, *all*, anyway have an axis of power and if the spokes are not equally proportioned then the one carrying the most unequal pressure may break and that's going to affect the relationship. New-millennium relationships must re-define themselves as bilateral beneficiaries and learn to be clear about how to work to empower and strengthen each other. People should avoid relationships if that relationship is going to weaken their mate. To me, that's the bottom line. Any type of friendship ought to be a strengthening relationship. If not, there's going to be abuse.

Let's go back a moment to something very foundational. No one can really love anybody without a sense of responsibility, without a sense of caring for another's condition. And further, responsibility grows out of a sense of spirituality. In essence, when we talk about spirituality or the spiritual, we are really talking about the connectedness of things. Please don't confuse this with religions because then we are getting too much involved with the dogma and doctrines of specific spiritual systems. I'm speaking of spirituality out of the traditional African worldview based on the principle that all existence is energy and that everything emanates from a great and potent conglomerate of energy and that in this is the life and vitality of the cosmos. Therefore, if all is energy or a physical manifestation of that original energy then all in creation is related and connected and therefore interactive, even if the interaction is not observable to our consciousness. And any part of the dynamism of one part of creation therefore affects the dynamism of the rest of creation and potential creation. What is done to one aspect affects the other aspect as a pebble causes vibrations when thrown in a pond. As the old folk used to sum it up, "What goes around comes around." Embraced in all of this fundamental principle we can see then is the law of karma. But let's not go off into that.

So if everything is connected, everything is a part of one great system. Consequently, to care for myself, to be responsible for myself, I have to care for all existence. So it is then with humans who are, we must remember, first of all energy and are only secondarily material. For without first being energy, material cannot come into being. Thus, I am related to everyone I meet and everything around me. To damage anyone, whether intimate acquaintance or not, is to do damage in some way to myself even though I may have no consciousness of how it will affect me, and even though I may be under the illusion that I got away without being caught. And that's an illusion because we don't have a good understanding of the dimension of time nor a comprehension of the true time of life. Unfortunately, it is one of the limitations of our humanity that we don't possess enough self-restraint and discipline unless motivated by fear. Violence within the community, at any level will not be deterred until people are taken with enough fear of retribution, politically or spiritually. Human beings will not be conscionable toward one another unless they feel some kind of connection.

Take, for example, people who commit premeditated murder, for example, these folk driving through the streets shooting or involved in drug distribution. These people have developed a totally distorted view of who they are and of the fundamental nature of existence itself. They are absent of caring, void of responsibility, utterly bereft of the knowledge of the connectedness of things. And this is the heart of the matter of where good relationships start, whether conjugal, familial, communal, racial or what. From their earliest days children have to be taught a sense of responsibility by engendering within them a sense of how everything is connected, how everything belongs to one great system of which they can never escape being a part no matter how they may try.

You see, we use the word responsibility but we don't explain very well what it really means. And it is here and only here where good relationships start. All the rest comes after this. Oppressed people especially have to be aware of this or they'll destroy themselves as a reflex action of their oppression. People who do not understand this and are not ready to take the time to instruct by this vital law of the cosmos ought not to bear children. Which is part of the horror of babies having babies when they themselves have not come into a knowledge of this primal law of the cosmos. And what is any neighborhood to be without this, what is any family to be without this?

Let's follow a little the psychology that grows out of this. We might say that some people are so fraught with power-lessness and low self-esteem that they feel pushed to irre-sponsibility. And sure, psychologically that is what deter-mines the irresponsible behavior of a lot of folk. But we have to look carefully at the problems with powerlessness and low self-esteem. If we define power as something absolutely given to us by other humans and as something which originates absolutely with other humans and if we inculcate these concepts into our children, speaking of any humans as being the most extraordinarily powerful things around, then we have already set the trap for our children to fall into the abyss of feeling powerless and possessing low self-esteem.

Thus, we get back to this notion of cosmic energy as the true potent source of all things. If we teach our children that they come from this greatest source of power and being and that they are always connected to this source of power, then their sense of who they are as cosmic beings rather than as earth or terrestrial beings will heighten their self-esteem and sense of power because they will know, especially after they begin to learn to live consciously and intuitively in connec-tion with this source for guidance, that their self-definition is not to be determined by any race of humans. In teaching this, we have to be careful to try not to use the word GOD because this word is too tainted in Western history by an-thropomorphism or, to be put simply, by the fact that the

West has cast GOD too much in man's image. And this has
bred all sorts of problems with implications for race and
gender. For that reason, when we teach our children about
their connection with this Most Potent Source, we would do
better to use terms which are abstract like Cosmic Divinity,
Divine Source, Potent Conglomerate of Energy, etc. The
wisest and ancient guardians of sacred wisdom have always
tried to instruct us with this type of terminology to keep us
from putting limitations on divinity. Because when we place
limitations on divinity we necessarily place limitations on
our own creativity. This principle of teaching is there, over
and over, in the ancient wisdom.

**Q: There is a great deal of subtle and overt disillusionment
among our young people. Do you have anything more
specific you might say to them?**

A: Yes. I'd reiterate first that they should remember that
their source of origin is beyond human beings. And that
even if they don't have any earthly parents that they should
always keep connected with the divine source from which
their parents came since their parents and no humans are
the origin of being but are rather only vehicles of being. So
the fact is that they are never really powerless and anyone
who teaches this is teaching a distortion. It is very important
for oppressed people to be taught this in their earliest years
and it is very important that they remember it every waking
and sleeping moment of their lives. So we are never really
powerless; it is all a matter of discerning where your power

lies and of deciding how to get the most value from it.

The next thing I would say is that they should not let anybody fool them into thinking that they don't have a future. Their future is in every phase of life to come, and the important thing about the future is learning to prepare for it and learning how to take up where you left off. That's what the best life is, the growth of the spirit or soul toward fulfillment. The soul or spirit is that part of you which you feel to be greater than your body, the spark of energy through which you maintain your connection with the Divine Source.

Then I'd say that young people have to learn to appreciate the relation between fulfilling oneself and being ready to make personal sacrifices for that fulfillment. That is, I may have to give up having something now in order to prepare to have something greater down the road. This is an important matter of self-discipline. And it takes self-discipline to stay close to the Divine Source of your being and potency. It is horrible to see, for example, how some people won't even take an hour to register to vote or to go vote when other people have sacrificed their entire lives for that opportunity to be provided and have sometimes suffered brutal deaths and torturings and jailings. People take their own convenience too much for granted and have little feeling for the price paid or how the price was paid. But it's easy to lose things taken for granted, and then you'll suffer for it.

I'd say to them that they should remember that everybody in some shape or form is looking for the good life and that they too can find the good life but that the truly good life needs a good foundation built upon good cycles of preparation and development. But look for a good life that's sound, not one that's synthetic and fraught with liabilities like taking and dealing drugs. Part of the problem with the crack/cocaine epidemic that is destroying so many young people and their babies comes from looking for an easy way to the good and from imitating others who are walking on shaky foundations. As if cocaine itself wasn't addictive enough and destroying enough lives around us, what did we have to do, since we wanted to imitate others so much, but do something foolish like going and creating a worse cocaine, called a poor man's cocaine. All because we wanted to imitate somebody we thought was chic, somebody we thought was living the good life, but who was really destroying himself or herself through addiction! There's nothing magnificent about that. That's sad. It's tragic. If you're going to follow anybody, don't follow a flake.

And finally, I'd say to the coming generations, or to any generation, for that matter, that if they don't create an agenda and good foundation for their own destiny that they can be sure that somebody else out there will create an agenda for them! You can't build great strength at the last minute.

You know, Toni Morrison is right when she says that it takes not simply parents but a community to raise a child. This concept which she is using is very important in traditional African culture. However, Morrison seems to think and advocate (in her 1989 interview in TIME Magazine) that because people are biologically ready to produce children that they are also ready to be parents. But bearing children and parenting are not exactly the same thing. And people in traditional African societies did not generally think that one's biological maturity meant that one was ready to be a parent. They didn't confuse biological develop-ment with responsible adult development. Therefore, in many, many African groups chastity was heavily enforced until marriage. And in some groups where pre-marital sex was allowed, those engaging in it were still forbidden to conceive a child until they had passed through their adult initiation stages. Sometimes the punishment could be quite severe for breaking these codes. Traditional African social codes were very sophisticated, so we have to be very careful about simplifying them. I think it would serve us well to study sexual behavior in some of the traditional African groups because among other things they could teach us a lot about discipline and birth control methods, all of which we could readily use in these times—and which we especially need.

Q: Before I forget, are we still dealing with the issue of teaching black English in the schools?

A: I think the most important factor here is that the teach-ers should know black English in order to know better how to teach standard English. That is, the teacher needs to know the child's language pattern in order to communicate and understand the child more effectively. The language pattern one learns to think and speak in is very important to their sense of self, and we have to keep this in mind and try not to snatch away someone's dialect but let them know that what we are trying to do is to give them another dialect or language pattern which they can use to present themselves and their thoughts in other situations. So more emphasis should be placed on language as a way of enhancing one's options and therefore of enhancing one's power. In this respect, we need to remember the ancient and traditional African cultural emphasis on the mastery of language. We need to be informed that it is not only in America that judgment is made of people by the language they use. This is also a major African tradition that carries very significant political and philosophical import. We need to have our language pattern respected, but let's not just settle for one language pattern. That would be very detrimental. We need to remember, too, that because Africans lived near African groups who spoke numerous other languages, they took it for granted that they might have to learn more than one language or language pattern.

Q: Do you think the black christians will have trouble with your recommendation that the term God not be used?

A: I imagine they will because christians have trouble with a lot of things. That's because they are so caught up in doctrines that other *men* have made and have sometimes instituted through physical and mental torture. Black christians need to develop a new courage of the spiritual intellect. The christians have trouble with a lot of righteous things, you know, because they often confuse their christian allegiance with the ideal ethical life and vice versa. Christian history itself should be enough of an indictment against such usage.

And black Americans ought to know this better than any-one else but are also the purveyors of this false synonymous usage. Christianity is not to be equated with the ethical life. Christ is a guide to and model for the ethical life but christianity is not!

The language of evangelization of christianity especially needs to be examined by black folk who, because they are often so afraid to critique the language and the doctrine, take the historical christian language as perfect without learning how to break the language down philosophically and etymologically in order to convey the very profound meanings that *are* at the depths of the words of the gospels. How are you going to convert or turn around someone if you don't understand the fundamental transformative dynamics and transference potency of the language you are using? When we translate the modern Bible back through the prism of its ancient African spiritual and philosophical ori-gins, for example, we learn that "Love thy neighbor as thy self" means much more than treat your neighbor as you would like to be treated or even as you love your self. This has to be broken down; it doesn't just speak for itself because when you look at life you see that it's horrible the way some people express love of themselves. In this great precept Jesus of Nazareth is making a statement from the point of view of a highly trained priest of the mysteries of the cosmos. He is speaking out of a knowledge of the unity of the universal energy force and what he was saying was that thy neighbor *is* thyself.

But most christians, black folk included, think and have been taught that it's blasphemous and heretical to go through

Africa to get to an understanding of Christ. And as long as they think that they'll never get to the true power of the WORD because the root of the word of Christ is in the great mystery schools of Africa, from the Jewish Torah to the four gospels. Most of this christianity that's being taught is just a cornflakes religion, an instant breakfast. They've looked all over the grits and butter. These black christians need to take up from where the Africans in America who composed the spirituals left off. They want to preach the word but don't really want to work to find out the meanings of the word. And suppose I suggested that you ultimately would have to go through a phase of Buddhism before you could really be free to be in heaven!! Well, I shouldn't say too much . . . You know there is the parable about the wine skins, so I'd better stop there.

But on another line, some of these preachers have become masters of running folk away from the churches and in the most crude ways. Instead of making the people feel spiritually comfortable so they will want to come back again, through religious inquisition they make the people uncomfortable, imposing on them to come forward and join the church then and there. You see they are working under the presumption that they who are in the church are the ones who are in the best ethical position to judge, but what they don't know is that they are also being judged and that's probably why the majority of the people won't return, they can not put their faith in the preacher's leadership abilities.

Something which needs to be seriously addressed by the christians is why the language and the rituals that they use alienates males. Go to any church and three-fourths to four-fifths of the congregation will be female. Male preachers head the churches but it is really women who compose it. But why is the Islamic mosque full of men at prayer hours? How can one claim to be a highly ethical being and not deal with addressing the challenge of the *absent* community?

From Phillis Wheatley in the 1800s down to contemporary young black preachers, we can see that Afro-America is still very much under spiritual blackmail. It is amazing how traditional still are the young black preachers in their relationship to the canon of Christian scriptures. While one hears and sees more of general African pride, few make use of or give validation to traditional African spiritual wisdom; few make attempts to incorporate any of the other universal spiritual wisdom of the various world religions.

The ministers seem therefore under the spiritual blackmail of Christianity, not though as set forth by Jesus of Nazareth who was really speaking of the higher and fundamental mysteries of life via parables and proverbial statements, but are still under spiritual blackmail of the European church fathers. This blackmail by the European church fathers is particularly apparent when one considers the enormous emphasis African Americans have placed and still place on the Old Testament. In thinking of the scores of sermons I have heard over the past forty years of my life, and in thinking of the scores of black churches of all denominations I have attended in states ranging geographically from Georgia to New Jersey, from Connecticut to Indiana, from Arkansas to northern and southern California, I have never heard any ministers make a reference to the Jewish keys (the Kabala, for example) for assistance in interpreting the Old

Testament scriptures.

This is tragically ironic since these scriptures are first of all records of Jewish spiritual history which the Jewish people have given so much attention to over the centuries, rigorously pursuing these texts for their higher, more profound, and emblematic meanings in connection with human physical and metaphysical life. This lack of attention or cowardice to give attention to the Jewish textual interpretation of Old Testament scriptures signifies a terrible blind spot in our engagement with and supposed use and adoption of that tradition. Nevertheless, African Americans refer to their spiritual and intellectual involvement with Christianity as Judaeo-Christian.

That African American preachers neglected the Jewish tradition of Old Testament interpretation accounts, I think, for some of the truly cultural thinness of African American ways of learning and knowing and knowledge systems, as well as the thinness of its maturation systems after the interference of slavery and racism with the continuation of the African systems. This neglect of Jewish interpretations of the scriptures also accounts for the almost too-easy way Christians, in general, buy into the notion of instant salvation, making it a kind of cornflakes religion. In addition, in the neglect by black preachers of the teachings of the ancient mystery school, epitomized by the mystery schools of ancient Egypt, from which Jesus of Nazareth received much of his initiation and training, can be seen a major cause of the Pauline-biased preaching that takes place in our churches placing so much emphasis on the crucifixion.

In essence, the great majority of the would-be-enlight-

ened young African American christian ministers are really
no greater than the best African American christian ministers like the late Rev. Junius C. Austin of Pilgrim Baptist
Church in Chicago. Yet these younger black preachers really think they are a new breed by virtue of their declared
willingness to be politically or socially involved. The fact is
that the young black preachers are rarely enlightened enough
regarding what their congregations desperately need to know
about the development of the spiritual intellect. They emphasize the ethical in a very provincial sense while almost
always overlooking the significance given by Jesus of Nazareth
to knowing and understanding as a component of the great
key to existence and the key to ultimate human liberation.
Even in the positive-thinking methods adopted by many of
the "progressive" African American ministers, these ministers are nevertheless working within the boundaries set by
the European and American Church Fathers' tradition.

Involved in this is a definite line of spiritual blackmail to
which African American ministers have subscribed. That
blackmail has been working for a very long time, at least
since the moment Phillis Wheatley understood that in her
adopted household Africa was a pagan land and therefore as
pagan possessed no worthy spiritual heritage. In a similar
way, it is as if since some Jews were said to be responsible for
the crucifixion of Jesus then there was nothing of worth in
Jewish scriptural interpretation. That's what I mean by spiritual blackmail!!

Q: A lot of references are made to ancient Egypt as a symbol of African achievement...

A: We have to be careful about our own contradictions, though. That is, we can't celebrate the glories of pharaonic Egypt and forget the bondage of the Jews while at the same time we clamor against our own bondage and even more contradictorily use the biblical history of the Jews as the major analogue to our travails. Sometimes you hear these contradictions out of the same mouth. That to me connotes a problematic, undiscriminating mentality which will in time generate and perpetrate other troubling, misleading contradictions. It asks the question of our sincerity about such things as *justice*. Is it justice we are seeking to establish or simply justice for ourselves? This is a very complex historical example which we use to serve dual purposes, even myself at times, I imagine. Nevertheless, it's important for us all to take heed of the ancient Egyptian premise given to the initiates in pursuit of higher truth, "Know thyself and then ye shalt know the gods."

Personally, I love studying about ancient Egypt and other ancient cultures. I wish I had more time to give to it. But there is a real danger out there in making so many references to the glories of ancient Egypt in the same way that there is danger in being blinded by any type of glory. In referring to Egypt, people so often come away with the superficial message of the achievements really of an empire, and to me this is only constructing a materialist analogy which ends thus in a celebration of *things* rather than in a celebration or comprehension of spiritual and intellectual discipline. These latter were the real achievements of ancient Egypt.

Thus, if people are sincerely inspired about ancient Egypt, they ought to be studying to master the laws and the principles upon which these ancient Africans were able to build a civilization that lasted for several thousand years. I mean somebody who leaves a lecture inspired by ancient Egyptian accomplishments ought soon thereafter to be involved in studying Egyptian mathematics, geometry, medicine, etc. This should especially be expected of our college students who like to bring up Egypt in the classroom but have not pursued and are generally not intending to pursue any primary study of Egypt's great wisdom. They quote secondary sources who are often quoting secondary sources. I don't see much interest in them of getting to the heart of the matter to study the languages and other disciplines which would help them to speak authoritatively on the subject. Therefore, they wouldn't be able to do much in an argument with someone who is out to refute ancient Egyptian achievement. When I see this happen over and over, I am bothered.

I'm bothered most of all because there is no real evidence of sincerity in the area. Not enough want to do the hard and grinding work. I am also bothered because these superficial citations, to me, point toward something these students are not aware of, and that is that what they are really celebrating is the idea of empire, not Egyptian intellectual and spiritual accomplishments. And I'm distrustful of people like this because what it really means is that they are primarily motivated by power—and that can be dangerous, especially when people think they are being motivated by something more noble. You watch some of these same people

who are supposedly celebrating Africa and they just overlook all the people living in thatched huts who may very
well be the best embodiments of human dignity and wisdom
that anyone will ever find. It's because the minds of these
students are actually still being controlled by imperial forms,
the same forms which placed us in the historical predicament in which we find ourselves.

We have to be careful to notice that we may often be
confusing our celebration of Africa with what may really be
a middle-class American identity crisis. I think Africa de-
serves better than that because of the richness of its cultural
legacy. Again, talk is cheap. Anybody can wear a pendant of
the continent of Africa around their neck.

Another thing that's being bantered about is the somewhat specious generalization that we are not a minority. It's
all right to talk about not being a minority in the global
arena. In the world we are not a minority, but in the United
States we are, and we have to remember both in order to
determine our political and economic strategies. If one mis-
applies the fact that in the world we are not a minority, then
it becomes easy to follow a fallacious logic that black nation-
alist parties can be politically triumphant on the national
level in the United States. Perhaps they can be victorious in
some communities where there are majority concentrations
of blacks, but beyond that it's a fool's errand.

On the larger level, African Americans are going to
have to be involved in sophisticated coalition politics. Don't
be so foolish to expect white people, especially, to trade one
brand of racial politics for another. And here's where I think
Lenora Fulani is making a classic mistake, as intelligent as

she is and as attractive as she is simply as a political candidate. She can't be victorious on the national level by leading a *black* party when blacks are in the minority. I would really be frightened if I saw the majority of Americans support such a ticket because I'd suspect that they had some ulterior motive. We need justice politics not racial politics. Thus, we have to be shrewd and sophisticated every mile of the way and maintain the poise and tenacity to challenge the arena. Lenora Fulani is good and could really draw a lot of support from all segments of the population if she would speak with greater emphasis on the people-nation. Fulani is the best of the un-elected that I know.

Q: Do you think that we have any more heroes to give our children now?

A: You know that was one of the big questions since the 1960s. It is always coming up. But it seems to me that we've long had great heroes. And we need to remember this, that the heroes are *there*. It is we who are not being heroic in that we are not giving them to our children. We have inventors, scientists, liberators, scholars, artists, writers, athletes and all. To wait for someone else to give our heroes to our children will indeed be the key to our undoing. The most important lessons of self-concept are to be taught in the home and the *caring* community. Yes, we need representation of our heroic accomplishments in the text-books because not only black children but all American children need to know about their American heroes of all races.

Yet, I'm always astounded that some of the people who are the first to talk about the deeply racist nature of this society also expect it to give us our heroes. I guess the expectation is just one of the paradoxes of thought that can exist in a "racist democracy," so to speak. One of our ground rules ought to be that we, from the outset, have in our homes books that we read and give to our children about African and African American heroes. And all of us need to have in our homes Vincent Harding's *There Is A River*, and read it. Now that's a legacy that we can stand on. And it's a discriminating legacy, pointing out the strengths and the weaknesses of our historical heroism.

We at least ought to go to the library and get some books. And if we don't have them in our library or bookstore we can look them up in *Books in Print* and order them or ask the library to do so. There are no excuses. And if we can't do this we don't need any children. It *is* better to light a candle than to curse the darkness! I don't intend to sit around on panels and at conferences to hear people talk about the same issues from one generation to another if they aren't going to shed new light on the problem and advance the argument. If you keep talking about the same thing without advancing the argument or shedding new light, then you are losing your potential audience and are demoralizing the ones who are trying to support you. From one month to another people talk about issues without adding anything new, instead of reassembling to evaluate the successes and failures of the solutions employed. That's the only way to strengthen the group. Otherwise, we're just creating a sense of bad faith about our own capabilities.

Q: A lot of political candidates of all races are vying for some of the black votes now. Do you think this helps our political leverage?

A: Yes, but we have to be discriminating enough to always be on guard for people of any race who are in pursuit of power to a greater extent than they are in pursuit of justice. I say this because power is ego-centric and therefore corruptive whereas justice is public-centered. It is power that corrupts justice, and one doesn't need dominion over something or someone to pursue justice. One only needs strength to pursue justice. The notion of dominion is always dangerous. And it's dominion that too many people want. And all of this should qualify the way we think about freedom. Freedom is a state of constant vigilance because it is part of the terribly imperfect nature of the human being to almost always want to curtail somebody else's freedom and to advance self-interest.

We have to always remember that freedom is no single momentary victory. That's what Frederick Douglass was trying to tell us in My Bondage and My Freedom. Freedom is always a matter of degrees of achievement. This is a very essential part of a worldview which we have to adopt and always live with. We have to live with it in the same way that we live with the fact breathing is a necessity of life. That is, that one breath does not give you eternal life! The struggle for freedom has to become a part of our automatic reflexes. There is no need of getting tired and weary about this any more than we get tired of breathing. It's just a vital function.

Q: How do you suggest we put this into effect?

A: How do we put this into effect? Scribble notes to our congressmen and other elected officials to let them know not only what we are thinking but also to let them know that we are watching them. The note doesn't have to be anything fancy, formal, or elaborate. They'll get the message. At the same time, we need to use all of our money power. We do not own very much in the marketplace but we do buy a lot and it is that which keeps the marketplace alive.

Watch the commercials to see who is sponsoring negative images and inscriptions of blacks on television and the rest of the media and send a short note or post card to the sponsors saying you are going to think twice before buying any more of their products or services and that you're going to tell your friends to think twice, too. Don't just watch what is shown but who is sponsoring it. Watch to see how many blacks are employed at the places we spend our money, not only employed at the check-out counters but in the offices upstairs and in the back. Electoral pressure and monitoring the money that comes into and out of our households and communities are probably the two most fundamental lessons that we learned as a result of our struggles in the 1950s and 1960s. These lessons were our greatest rewards and they helped take our struggles and life activity to a new level of sophistication. These lessons told us not just to vote but told us how to use the vote, not just to increase our economic standard but how to put economics to work. We must never retrench on these lessons. We don't always have to be losing ground.

We have to remember that we're in a country dominated by a people who believes itself to be a christian nation on the one hand, but also believes in the survival of the fittest on the other hand. This dual, contradictory belief system can confound the expectations of anyone living in their midst if not aware that a dual belief system is always at work. This dual, contradictory belief system is an irreconcilable paradox that informs the American psychological behavioral problem. It means they are perennially involved in a juggling act with anyone over whom they think they have dominion. That's why the pendulum swings as it does back and forth, in one direction now and another direction tomorrow. And we're one of the balls or bowling pins being juggled about. But we don't have to be inert balls or bowling pins. That's for sure.

Part of learning to be masters of ourselves and of our destiny is in learning to be masters of adversity. That's the reality. And one cannot move until one acknowledges the reality. And there's a difference between acknowledgement of reality and acceptance of it. The first is a matter of sizing up the situation in order to know how to act; the second is more ambiguous in that it can suggest resignation. That's why I use the former.

I was saying before that a terrible unconscious fallacy is sometimes at work in our minds. That is, in thinking that because we're victims we are de facto good. We must beware of this fallacy which can dig a trap for any oppressed group. The fallacious logic is extended to thinking that because we are oppressed we are good and when we become liberated we are only capable of producing good. I don't know where this

line of thinking came from. One thing I do know and that is
that it didn't come out of the great knowledge and wisdom of
Africa. Africans have always had a more sophisticated understanding of human beings than that. This kind of fallacious reasoning sets us up to be "surprised by sin," as Milton
would say, surprised by our own egotism. It's imperative that
we study the ancient African legends as handed down through
Africans so that we'll know better how to define ourselves,
so that we won't be led to romanticizing ourselves. It will
save us a lot of trouble and prevent a lot of collective
demoralization down the road.

Life is more cosmically complex than to be thinking of
ourselves in simple-minded terms. All of that is, of course, a
deep metaphysical subject which has to be taken up in
another context. Nevertheless we must not fall prey to that
fallacy—because it carries with it its own terrible logic that
if I the victim am the good then I am incorruptible by power,
that I am virtually invulnerable to the deadly sins and the
temptation of power. Thus, when so many people talk about
revolution they are really talking about inverting the order
of dominance. And because they equate their victimization
with their goodness (again falling into the categorical fallacy
that the oppressed are the good and the oppressors are the
bad, forgetting the single-most important thing, that all
oppression is bad and the only thing worth pursuing is
justice), they think that power in their hands will be okay.
Further, I think the reason they think in terms of inverting
the order of things is because they are actually intellectually
too lazy to create a new order!

And there's a complementary fallacy attached to that

one. That is, that just because someone is oppressed they are ready for revolution. There is a real difference between needing something and being ready to undertake acquiring it. The important thing before revolution is that the oppressed be made aware not simply of their oppressors but of the nature of the oppressive structure which is set in place to facilitate and manipulate oppression. This is important because, again, the fallacy is that so often when people say that they want change they mean, often without knowing it, that they desire what their oppressors have. When really the only desire, the ultimate desire of a people-nation (to use Gramsci's term) should be justice and functional equality which provides and protects the access of everyone to the seed and fruits of the nation.

The African American, (and *all* future Americans) in order to be triumphant, is going to have to make a leap of consciousness. That is, we cannot fall into despair simply because the historical epoch will not allow us to move into or gain fulfillment based on the old American dream, the capitalist, materialist mode of fulfillment; for that epoch is at its close; destroyed by its own aggrandizement, by its own privileging of aristotelian logic which posits too much value on the working of the brain and eschews the more profoundly beneficial model of the spiritual-intellect.

Q: How do we avoid increasing the ranks of what is now called the underclass?

A: I think that we must be careful not to help ourselves

become impoverished. I think the first thing to remember is that capitalism is not an economic system put in place to look out for the needs of everybody. And since this is a capitalistic democracy that also means that the government is not going to look out for the needs of everybody. So, from the start one has to develop his or her survival and economic mobility strategies with this in mind. It doesn't mean that one has to accept this as the economic order which one believes in but one certainly needs to know what one is dealing with in order to be able to survive to challenge it. So I would recommend several basic and fundamental strategies to be used not singly, if possible, but in concert like a battalion in order to avoid falling into this so-called underclass status and increasing its ranks. Some of these points are reiterations of what I have already said.

I think the first thing I would say is to ground yourself in a spiritual philosophy which stimulates you, which motivates you and makes you feel good, and use it. We all need spiritual systems to help us avoid adversity and to help us to deal with adversity when it arises. Try to link yourself with some group that shares your belief system, and, moreover, work with that group. Probably nobody is going to find a group which is exactly perfect, but most of us can find a group, formal or informal, with which we can work toward common goals. People who belong to networks like this usually look out for each other in that they keep their eyes open for opportunities which will help their associates and friends. And this is the way that things work in all levels of life.

A good spiritual system or positive belief system is the

motor of life, and it is only this that can keep one from becoming impoverished even if one virtually has nothing material to lay claim to. But it is a positive belief system that helps one to maintain the inner poise to spring back and to wrestle with and overcome adversity. It is this that keeps us from worsening our condition in allowing ourselves and families and neighborhoods, for example, to be given over to litter as if we don't live there. Maybe it is someone else's house where you live and you just pay rent, but it is your home. And hygienic conditions have a powerful impact upon a person's sense of dignity and self-worth. We must always keep ownership of our own dignity, at whatever cost; that's something one never should let anyone else control.

Secondly, I would say that we have to be careful to let our true needs dictate our desires, and not the other way around. That is, the outer world makes an occupation of trying to create in us unnecessary desires. And if we go in constant pursuit of these desires then we so often forget our true needs. By true needs I am referring to things of substance which we can use to give us greater strength, which we can use to build on. For example, I mean, why spend four dollars for a carton of soft drinks when that same money could be much better spent on several quarts of milk which will be infinitely more valuable to strengthening your family's health and therefore their ability to deal with life's challenges?

Why spend three dollars for a bag of potato chips with little nutritional value when for probably a cheaper price you can buy several bunches of collard greens or several bags of carrots? Why spend four dollars for a box of cornflakes when for a cheaper price you can get five pounds of grits and some eggs to provide a breakfast that will contribute substantially to your family's well-being? What I mean is that we have to be careful because what we'll often find is that the things that we don't need cost us more than the things we need. People just don't know how they let television commercials determine their behavior, and, to their detriment. They need to take television for just what it is — an exploitative illusion to make money for somebody else at whatever cost to you, meaning even your life. You can't raise healthy children off cornflakes illusions. They need the basics. I think it's from television that people get these bad eating habits.

And thirdly, I'd emphasize that we always should be on the look out for ways to improve and build the basic educational skills of ourselves and our families, and should always be looking for ways to develop our individual talents. This is one of the main ways to remain functional, to have a service to offer to someone else in exchange for which we can get the money we need to acquire our needs.

Politically speaking, I would say, too, that it's outright foolish and self-defeating to give in to the notion that one or two particular groups already have the American vote in their pocket. American politics has a lot of variants which change from season to season, era to era. But people make the seasons and the eras. And these variants come together around various ideological, social, economic issues and causes to form alliances. And that's how winning is done.

Q: Are there any issues of self-concept which still need addressing?

A: Yes. Especially that of our natural appearance. There has certainly been an improvement of African American self-concept from the time when I was growing up in the 1950s and early sixties, but there is still great work to be done in getting young African descendants to see themselves and the features of their beauty, and the power of all that, from an African aesthetic or standard of beauty. We have to re-learn how to groom the African in us. This aesthetic should actually begin with a cultivation of good feeling about one-self from the inside and should radiate outward to an understanding of laws of proportion and harmony which govern African features. That is, we need to cultivate an appreciation of the sense that nature has in matching parts of the face by giving one, for example, a broad or rounded nose instead of a long thin pointed nose to match one's full lips. Moreover, too, many African American women still subject themselves to that very unnatural law that to be a real woman you should have long hair. That's a terrible psychological tyranny that causes many African American women to feel and look ugly. This is a tyranny that inflicts self-denial and consequently a denial to one's own natural self-affirmation, sense of power, and birthright.

Q: Can you explain more of what you mean by connecting self-denial to natural power?

A: Yes. If you worry too much about not fitting into the European standard of beauty, you raise your anxiety level and your constant level of stress significantly. Stress and anxiety sap your energy from you, and that means that you have less mental energy to do other things. That is, you short-change your natural energies because you are using up a lot of your personal energy or power in trying to hide from yourself. Thus, you have less power and poise for dealing with the world.

Q: Well, wasn't something like this revisory process begun in the 1960s?

A: Yes, but it was interrupted in symbolic representation by the transformation of the Jackson Five from the natural hair style to the jerri curl.

Q: But don't a lot of general Americans go through physical changes themselves? Don't they dye their hair, fix their noses, and eyes and lips?

A: Yes, if this wasn't so, Revlon and the cosmetic industries would be out of business tomorrow. Nevertheless, your true power is in grooming yourself around your natural characteristics, not around an artificial standard imposed by some outer force of manipulation of your self-concept. What I mean is, and this is the heart of the matter, is that you are fighting a daily battle with nature, and in waging this constant war from the moment you awake in the morning and look at the mirror you are beginning to waste an enormous amount of energy which could be given to performing other, more significantly rewarding tasks.

Every task, mental or physical, requires the expenditure of energy. A little girl or boy who is constantly worried, consciously or subconsciously, about his or her hair or features is burning energy that could be applied to learning and to training of themselves and to unleashing, harnessing and developing their talents. In fact, the battle with nature can sometimes be so consuming that the general energy level remains low and the person gives the appearance of being in perpetual dejection. So the deep secret to personal beauty and power is to work with your naturalness, to groom it and cultivate it because when you fight it or deny it you are blocking your energies. It's like having trash in your carburetor and the fuel can't get to the engine. You see too now why envy is considered one of the seven deadly sins?

Q: Are you surprised that so many black college students, especially on predominantly white campuses, seem disillusioned?

A: Partly not. It's like I said earlier: because college life is the first real moment when they confront the American dream for what it is. That is, they see clearly who is wielding the power and how that power is held in check and that race is one dimension of it. Not that they don't see something of all this earlier but they expect that the outside world is different from the idealized world of the university where presumably intelligence reigns. Sadly, though, this is not true, and their bubble is burst at the moment when they expect to make the wonderful and fulfilling transition into great American womanhood or manhood and get well on to the road of American success and upward mobility. They just knew that in their ideal intellectual environment of the university that genius would show itself, be acknowledged, and encouraged by all. That their mentors would be standing at the gate ready and waiting to receive them.

I think, though, that in looking for mentorship, acknowledgement, and encouragement from everybody in the university that students often tragically overlook a number of people who, in this time (both black and white) are indeed available to give them the assistance and guidance they need. One of the first things that any college student needs to know is that college professors, probably more than any other part of the population excepting entrepreneurs, believe in the survival of the fittest, and colleges and universities operate out of that mode. If you make less than a perfect score, many professors are not going to invite you to their offices to discuss your weaknesses. They expect that motivation to originate from within the student. So what I mean most by *fittest* here is that the personal motivation to pursue and inquire is probably what is going to determine who is fittest. You have to always, in any walk of life, affirm and believe in your own potential and be motivated by that and you can't forget, especially as an African American, that you have to think creatively about your own destiny. Don't expect your affirmation to come from a racist society. Acknowledge improvements in the society but remain circumspect until it makes a complete turn around.

And see, too, there is another problem that comes with this generation of college students. They came up thinking that they were really middle-class, and now they are confronting the real American upper middle-class, students whose parents control the modes of economic activity and make a lot of the profits, not just a salary out of which you can just barely meet your mortgage and other expenses. In addition, they may become aware of a class of students who will inherit enough money and assets to keep them well ahead of the pack. Many indeed will inherit more money than lots of us will ever earn. And African American students are being confronted with all of these realizations which have major ramifications for exercising control of their destiny.

One flaw, however, is that black students don't know how to put a lot of the advantages of white people into perspective. A major flaw is in lumping all white people together, to generalize that they are all in the upper middle-class when they are not. Most of these black students (and white students, for that matter) have never been in the homes of truly wealthy white people, particularly those who have been wealthy for generations, neither to visit nor to work, so they don't even have a good frame of reference for establishing in their minds who is to be envied, if there is ever any worth in envy at all.

Everybody who can take a vacation three times a year is not wealthy, you know. So a lot of the shock that these students are experiencing is a class shock as well as a racial shock. They're realizing they are not even as middle-class as they thought, as they had been mis-led to believe with all the generalized rhetoric about middle-classness that was so popular during the Reagan administration. If they haven't read much about the mentality of the middle-class, they'd better get busy and start reading the French plays of Moliere of the seventeenth century and then come on up and read E. Franklin Frazier's *Black Bourgeoisie* published in the United States in the 1950s. Otherwise, they'll be repeating a lot of tragic pitfalls of the middle-class. In fact, they are already repeating them.

For example, it is characteristic of new middle-class people to try to impress others; consequently, they engage in a lot of conspicuous consumption, spending money so that others will notice them (like spending too much on clothes and cars) instead of investing the money to help it multiply into something that will give them a greater power base. This is a characteristic pitfall which emerging middle-class people should watch out for in themselves. And as Professor Sylvia Wynter of Stanford is trying to emphasize, the people trying to rise from lower-middle class status can be influenced to perform some very ominous deeds. There's a dangerous psychology that can become operative when one is taken by this drive. It's easy to become a henchman or lynchman for the ruling classes, and the force is as operative in women as in men in all types of occupations and professions.

Comparative knowledge can be of great assistance to us

if we would use it to our advantages. I mean, even though our historical position is relatively unique, and we have to remember that, our historical situation is however not totally different from experiences with oppression that other groups have experienced in history from other racial groups and from their own racial groups. So we shouldn't speak or think simplistically about ourselves as if we are the only ones who have experienced anything like this.

We should study diligently other experiences as well as our own and use and compare experiences and strategies. And there is a lot that we can study with respect to racial and ethnic clashes and oppression, both political and economic, which can be quite informative from every continent on earth including Africa. Sometimes it seems that we think that if we could simply do away with our American oppression we would be free and powerful. But it's not that simple. Do you think that if we could set up a nation today on independent soil that the Soviet Union or China or some European nation or African nation would just let us be free plain and simple? It's simple-minded to think in that way. Very simple-minded. But it seems that lots of us think that way without realizing that we are thinking in a fantasy construct. And when you think in fantasy constructs that makes it all the more difficult to deal with your problems because what you are trying to do is not realistic.

Another thing: Don't let your sense of suffering overshadow the true reality of time and a reasoned perspective of it. Keep a sense of historical time in perspective, in your frame of reference. Don't let your sense of suffering overshadow your sense of time because suffering has a way of

making time seem very long. So don't be mesmerized by suffering. If you do it'll turn your dynamic-organic potential into a pillar of salt. Fifty or a hundred years can make a nation unrecognizable. Think of this, the Spanish had headway in imperial control of the American hemisphere for over a hundred years before England even got a foothold. Where is Spain today? Where is Portugal? Then remember this that English colonial domination of the now United States lasted not even two-hundred years. And now here we are a nation not much above two-hundred years old and are mired in deep economic and moral and structural trouble.

The economic structure is a fabrication, the physical foundation is plagued by pollution, and the metaphysical structure is polluted by too much hypocrisy and moral cowardice. Problems demand that changes take place in time; so time changes, but human beings must take on the responsibility to bring about the needed changes. You can never just sit by and let fate take its course because usually there is some other human being out there helping to determine the course of fate. A lot of us are operating from the worldview that the meek shall inherit the earth, or inherit the nation, etc., or from the view that the bottom rail will one day be on top. I really don't like that top and bottom type of thinking.

Why does anyone need to have power over someone else? That to me is different from empowerment. And, too, just because you inherit something doesn't mean that you have prepared yourself to keep it. You can inherit it today and lose it tomorrow. And, again, when considering racism, remember this and don't let anyone tell you any differently, that it is not because of their experience with black folk that white folk are afraid we might be vengeful because of the way they have treated us: their fear is really based upon white folk's own experience with white folk. Their frame of reference about the world and human nature is based primarily on their European relationship with each other, all of the centuries of warring and all. They're just projecting and transposing their worldview onto black folk who have never committed such horrendous atrocities against them as they have against each other. Keep that in mind when you are thinking about ethnic and racial psychology and motives. Don't be naive about European history. If you do, you're only helping the wizard and taking from your own strength.

Q: What are we going to do about so many of our young men, especially, getting caught up in the criminal justice system? And what can we do about the delinquent activity in our youth which is working to the detriment of our communities?

A: Let's start with the latter question. There is a certain percentage of children born into every human community, each neighborhood, who are inclined to be risk-takers, are inclined to risk danger. Parents and other nurturers have to recognize early that these risk-takers are not necessarily in their earliest stages manifesting delinquency, but are rather expressing a certain talent for risk-taking. You understand what I mean? Risk-taking is a talent. Now, which way that risk-taking is used is another matter. Thus, we have to prepare these talented people from an early age with all types of skills which they can use to have more options to nurture their particular talent, so that when they begin to grow up they won't be so easily lured off into unbeneficial, risk-taking adventures such as criminal activities. Children with risk-taking talents should be told early about risk-taking professions from which they can have a beneficial life, professions such as airplane piloting, engineering, deep-sea diving, movie stunt acting, and what ever else. All of this takes us back to the primary emphasis we need to place on observing human beings from before birth onward as energy forces and in naming the energy forces in a way to challenge and raise self-esteem rather than to negate self-esteem. Thus, why not call a young child who is inclined to go beyond boundaries a "risk-taker" and create positive challenges for him or her, rather than call him or her "bad" and immediately cultivate in them a negative psychology regarding their energy.

To add to that answer, I would say that you can judge what the quality of your community of the future will be by observing the level of responsibility existent in or being inculcated into the children and youth by the parents and other nurturers. You'd better work out some strategy to instill responsibility or otherwise you and your community are going to be in trouble. It is *only* the sense of responsibility that makes the qualitative difference in the life of a community. Everything else, material well-being and all, comes after that. For it is only a sense of responsibility that is the bottom line for overcoming and enduring adversities. Everything else is superficial to responsibility. The most important, most valuable legacy that can be given to a child or youth, rich or poor, is a sense of responsibility. A poor child not given a sense of responsibility will never overcome the obstacles; a rich child not given a sense of responsibility won't be rich long. A classic fault in rising middle-class families is that their children often focus more on their privileges than on their responsibilities and therefore are not making preparation to leave a worthwhile legacy, economic, political or whatever for the next generation. As the old folk used to say, "Mark my word!" I know from observation that it is the worst mistake to believe that just because you are a hard working parent your children will automatically emulate your sense of responsibility. Responsibility is something that has to be talked about, taught, and inculcated.

There is one main tragedy of the mind which for whatever reasons moves toward delinquency or criminality. That is, the delinquent or criminal mind mis-weighs its options, although the options may be few. What kind of lasting reward can ever come to oneself, one's family, and one's friends through delinquent activity? That is what has to always be kept in mind when people feel themselves inclined in those directions. The self, the family, and friends pay a heavy price once that option is taken. Even if others are being unjust to us let us not be unjust to ourselves. It's like putting more pressure on the dagger that's in your chest or the boot that's on your neck.

Another problem is that the person who sees himself or herself as the victim of abuse so often has a first response of wanting to abuse or take advantage of someone else. We have to resist that first response because it has no long-term rewards and it only gets us caught up in a vicious cycle, and

when in this cycle one seeks opportunities for abuse. This mentality even more tragically sees kindness and humility as an opportunity to exploit and abuse, for example. Whereas, it ought to be challenging itself instead to use these as opportunities for regeneration and worthwhile or longstanding rewards. So the key is that one who finds himself or herself inclined toward delinquency or criminality is going to have to learn to catch themselves when they find their minds wandering into this tragically punitive mode. Because if you don't learn how to use opportunities for longstanding rewards, then you're dooming yourself and probably the others who care about you. So it has a lot to do with how we treat options or opportunities. The cycle within the self has to be broken. Ernest Gaines wrote a very good story about this called "Three Men." It's published in his collection called *Bloodline*. It's a good story and is very insightful and instructive.

Don't fall for the notion that you only live once and that when you're dead you're done. That's a destructive view of time. I don't think that came out of African wisdom at all. And how we view time plays a major role in determining all our behavior patterns. When we get caught up in thinking that we have only one chance or time to do something, we trap ourselves into the mode of immediate gratification rather than in seeking the longstanding reward. If we are going to become involved in high risk activities, let us get involved in some that are really productive. Otherwise, we're not as daring as we think ourselves to be. Anybody can do something that can lead to a prison sentence. Anybody. Let's not forget that a lot of what we've been experiencing in America is a great con game, the experience of a performing confidence man in his masquerade. That's a basic part of what has shaped the core of the American identity. Not only has the victimized black used subterfuge in the role of the trickster, but the dominant white society has played and still plays the role of the trickster, too. We must not forget that, and must therefore feel obliged to be as wise as serpents.

Q: What are your general basic recommendations for African Americans?

A: Well, I have several sets. One has to do with developing our minds, sense of self, and basic sense of destiny and dignity.

We must cultivate our own magnificence as an African people by nurturing and building a stronger learning culture. The magnificence which is within each of us is waiting to be developed and brought forth by us, for us, for our own enhancement and the enhancement of the world. We must make a *cultural habit* of employing, examining, creating, and partaking of learning systems which will stimulate our magnificence. This can be done in many ways. And we should work to employ a combination of ways, including the reading of books! Learning from books how other people have dealt with certain issues can save us a lot of trial and error. We may not necessarily find all of the answers but we can certainly find some by reading about other people's thoughts and experiences.

You know, people often think they don't have time to

read books. Well, you don't have to read the whole book in one sitting, nor in one week, nor in one month. Books can be read a few pages or paragraphs at a time. So we need to take more advantage of the written word. It can be a good resource holding a lot of valuable information and insight. We must not worry much about being rewarded by the outside world. A cultivation of the magnificent within our-selves must become the first dignity principle which we embrace and through which we reward ourselves.

Rewards from the outside world for our own cultural cultivation of the magnificent must not be more than sec-ondary in our motivations and expectations. Our motiva-tions and expectations must be primarily self-rewarding be-cause the use of a self-rewarding system is the only way we can gain and retain ownership and mastery of our dignity and destiny. When one first expects one's cultivation of the magnificent to be rewarded by outsiders, then one does not wish to own oneself and one becomes a force in his or her own destruction and subjugation. Whether we own or dwell in a single geographical territory or not, we can still create a magnificent nationhood within our minds, which, by the way, may be the safest place for a nation to be kept.

To bring out the magnificence within oneself does not mean that one has always to be perfect, but it does mean that one possesses a very high regard and a very high degree of gratitude for the innate magnificence which one has been given at birth. Being magnificent means that one is working to perform always at a very high standard in honor of the creative force which is within, which generated us, and which will continue to regenerate us as long as we acknowledge this force by periodically cultivating it and by using it well—whether we are developing as electricians, carpenters, mathematicians, beauticians, nurses, mechanics, artists, linguists, philosophers, plumbers, theologians, chemists, or whatever. The cultivation of the magnificent must become an essential part of the momentum of our basic existence in respect to our personal selves, families, neighborhoods, and larger communities. This is basic to our survival and endurance.

We need to redefine ourselves in a number of ways, or more emphatically, we need to think about *how* we define ourselves and about how we allow ourselves to be defined. A good example of this is that one of the key issues or problems that we have relates to the re-genderization of African culture by the European influence. I mean for instance like what happens to dance in the United States. Dance becomes more closely labelled "feminine," and/or becomes associated with gender designations and gender activity. Thus, an important part of the male African cultural birthright is given up. But given up in exchange for what? The power of being free to dance was given up for what? What was it exchanged for? Further weakening? Emasculation? What did the black male get in exchange? We have to remember that the primary and essential association of dance in traditional African culture is a way of making a ritual connection with the great empowering forces and Great Conglomerate Force of the cosmos. But what happens when black men begin to think of dance as "feminine," as something that belongs most to womanhood? Do black American men yet have, en masse, as powerful a substitution for that

which they gave up for connecting with the Force?

Which brings us to a similar and major problem with spirituality. And this is really now at a tragic crisis point, the way young men are murdering each other and their communities. It's a lack of spirituality, a desperate lack of connectedness to other human beings. Spirituality, too, is seen by black men in the United States too much in terms of being "feminine." The nature of the religious encounter with Christianity in the West is, of course, largely responsible for this in the way that it was used as an oppressive and emasculating force during slavery and its aftermath. Christianity, in general, has become paradoxically linked with women even though its principal historical figures have been male.

The sad thing is that we have come to tyrannize and destroy our own selves through these Western genderizations, categorizations, and labellings of being. We won't let ourselves *be* for trying to be what someone else says we should be. This goes over into the area of our personal aesthetics even, black women sometimes denying themselves their natural beauty because somebody else says women are supposed to wear their hair long. Look at how soon it takes over the lives of little black girls. And look how their self-esteem falls down, down, down because of that. See how we can screw ourselves up? We end up functioning as the officers of our tyranny once the oppressive design has been set in motion.

Next I would say that it should not be expected that we can grow from generation to generation unless we first develop and nurture in our children a sense of responsibility and conscience with respect to themselves and their world.

It should not be expected that we can grow from generation to generation with fathers who can spend hours several times a week looking at sports games (cultivating an illusion of manhood) but who will not give an hour a night to make sure their children learn how to read, write, count, and think well before they finish high school. It is not to be expected that we will improve from generation to generation if we do not take our own situation and our own suffering seriously enough to devote time to teaching and providing discipline and skills to the coming generations. Generations always need discipline, skills, and a sense of responsibility so that they can not only take advantage of new opportunities but so that they can become shrewd enough to learn how to *create* opportunities.

Probably the one thing that has gotten us into a greater depth of trouble than anything else in our history has been that so many people in this last twenty years have been taken in by the idea of making "easy money," which basically spells "drugs." That's the main reason why we've become so plagued by crime and murders within our communities; that's the main reason why so many of the more life-sustaining options for personal advancement are being undermined from the grade-school up. Some people adopted this "easy-money" worldview, they thought, as a way of scoffing at this unjust system, not to change it.

The only one benefiting from "easy-money" is the pernicious system itself. We've hi-jacked ourselves and have come out far worse with seemingly unending worries. Not to take anything away from the very perniciousness of racism as it infects and affects the American way of life, let's remember as Ned Cobb said in *All God's Dangers* that "all of God's dangers ain't necessarily the white man." The biggest danger is always the self and how the self responds to various situations, including racism. That's where the key is, in the self and how it responds. That is, whether the self responds out of naivete, stupidity, cynicism, or sophistication.

You know, I find it very interesting that in the rhetoric of a lot of people spouting off about racism is buried the expectation that those same people they label as the oppressor ought to be motivating them. I hear it often, blaming someone you say hates you for not motivating you and your children. This kind of confused logic and language tangles peoples emotions and makes them still incapable of being motivated. Such talkers only further complicate the lives of the people. These type people are not leaders; they are traitors. There is no need to continuously preach about the condition, unless that condition needs to be re-defined (which is important to be done often) but what's important is to come up with and give varieties of antidotes, strategies, and options for alleviating and undermining the condition and the poison.

We have to remember one very important thing about *motivation*. That is that motivation is always related to rewards and reward systems, either external or internal ones. By motivation is meant one is "moved" by something —a desire, a yearning, a cause, or whatever. Oppressed people have to be very careful not to sit and wait in expectation of getting positive motivation from individuals seen as representing the oppressor, what I call the force of the outer head. It's foolish to think otherwise. And it's very defeating to think of all white people as representing racism and racist oppression.

When people become very cynical and hopeless, it's because they are putting too much trust in easy thinking. We always have to think complexly, using the inner head as the buffer and the gauge, not the superficially-oriented outer head. Only complex thinking is the way to work through a lot of these complex issues even though complex thinking is going to be generally more painful. But we have a formula for that, too, forged by our ancestors as a way of instructing us on how not to be done in by pain. That's what they talked about in the blues and folktales.

It's so easy to undermine your own energy, your own motivation. I remember talking to a very nice young engineering student who was having some difficulties with course work, trying to encourage him to organize study groups among his peers so that they might help enlighten each other and cover more of the assignments, but he kept focusing so much upon the *possible* obstacles, and more than that he kept focusing so much on the advantages, resources, knowledge, and expected performance some of the white students had come to the University with that he couldn't see the resources that existed within his own group. A lot of his energy was being burned up in his anxiety about his disadvantages, and it undermined his motivation and level of performance. That same energy burned up in anxiety could have been used to develop strategies for performance. He couldn't see that his present experiences, even though they were very trying and disappointing at times, if analyzed properly, could be used to great advantage if he would pinpoint the basic problems, then focus on developing strategies and antidotes for combatting the problems. He could also use his knowledge of certain problems to be ready to alert the next group of freshmen to what they ought to be prepared to tackle and to suggest some strategies for doing that. But this student's *reaction* to the problems became greater than the problems themselves. That is, he got so mesmerized by the problems and the conditions that he couldn't think his way out of them in a timely fashion. So our way of reacting and of responding can sometimes be our greatest stumbling blocks.

It's of critical importance not to focus too much on the "advantages" of another person or group unless you are going to use what you are looking at to forge advantages for yourself. Otherwise, you are only raising the level of *negative anxiety* within yourself which will frustrate you so much that you become inhibited from performing at your best. So never focus upon the opposition or competition unless you are going to learn from it. Otherwise, your anxiety is blinding yourself to your own resources and advantages. Study the competition to stimulate strategies, not to heighten frustration. You can get so caught up in complaining that the negative reality you are focusing on overtakes your identity and determines your reality.

Let me tell you something: I had a professor once, who, though he was a nice man, could not tell me how to improve my writing style while he nevertheless criticized its weaknesses. Had I been a less self-reliant person, I could easily have let that man's own limitations as a professor decide my fate. But I saw those as his professional limitations, not as mine. He was being paid as the teacher, not I. So I took that aspect of my destiny into my own hands by taking the time to find out for myself what my problems were and how I could remedy them. That's the attitude I take toward racism and racists: I'm not going to sit by and be doomed by *their* psychological limitations. For I know that I can only win when I struggle, and when I struggle I can never lose because either way I'm going to end up feeling better about myself!! You can always do something to strengthen yourself. No matter how slight it is, you can always do something.

We must remember that the oldest trick of the poser of riddles is to put on an awesome face or to take on an awesome character. The reason for this is to confuse our energies, to thwart our clarity. No condition, no problem is permanently fixed. All things are subject to change. The key is that any problem, any condition, has to always be perceived as something that can be de-mystified. The aim of the wizard is to keep you mesmerized, to make your reasoning lose its fluidity and flexibility; so don't play into the wizard's game.

Just think, for example, of how bewildered and mesmerized some people get when they are constantly confronted with overwhelmingly negative statistics about the future of black males in America. They hear the statistics, give too much authority to the perpetrators and generators of the statistics, and instead of reasoning their way beyond the manipulations of the wizards, they lose their energy to depression instead of using the energy to open themselves up to the creation of strategies for dealing at various levels with the issues causing the problems. I think a lot of young people, and older people, too, don't understand the rhetorical or argumentative intent of the very tragic statistics. The main purpose that people use them is not so much to say that African descendants in America *are doomed*, but is rather to say that if we— each person, each parent, each family, and each community doesn't get some kind of enhancing act together, then we *are*_doomed. The future can be better if we work for it, but sitting and complaining is only going to further demoralize us. The same energy used to complain and gripe could be used to do something!

Some people love to hear the dire statistics of the soothsayers so that they can have another excuse not to be courageous, not to be holistically responsible. Save me from the complainers! Be constructive, be an analyst and a strategist. Why be negative when in the same moment with the same energy you can be positive? The key point is not to let racism undermine your sense of self-discipline, not to let racism make you stupid! If I'm going to be a victim, I'd rather be a victim with some skills which I can use to fight rather than allow myself to succumb totally to thoughts of victimization and become a demoralized piece of nothingness, complicating my own existence.

It should not be expected that we can fight well against the odds and the evils of life if we do not use our foresight to be prepared to face them. It should not be expected for good luck or good fortune to be of any use if we do not or cannot use the opportunity which fortune provides. And not using the opportunity is like spitting in the face of the spirit that has helped you. Part of the reason many youth lose out and cannot excel on the most competitive levels in the world is not because they are not smart enough but because they are not skilled, developed, or disciplined enough. A youth who does not go to school long enough to get a good understanding of the history of the world and how the world operates, will probably go through life feeling very much like a helpless victim.

Also, young sisters need to be told straightforwardly that it is more important for them to shape a good future and destiny than it is for them to help a young fellow to satisfy his sexual urges. Young brothers must be told and taught to find creative, un-risky ways to channel and release their biological impulses rather than take the unconscionable risk of producing a child whom they, for *any* reason, would be inclined to abandon or be unable to raise into a secure, prepared, and responsible adulthood. Young sisters must be told that it is wrong to conceive a child because they feel lonely and want the child to serve as company.

You know, I think some of us mis-identify having babies, lots of babies, with being African, as if there is some virtue simply in giving birth. But they've got that wrong! African culture has more wisdom to offer than that. Procreation is only emphasized in traditional African culture in marriage! And marriage means commitment. Never forget that African cultures are disciplined cultures! Unfortunately, because of slavery, a lot of us never knew that, and in not knowing that, that is one of the reasons why our self-esteem is often so low. I was just looking at the cover of a recent issue of *Ebony Magazine* featuring the cover story of what the young black professionals and leaders of the 1990s would look like. And what I saw on that cover was really tragic, because even though, you had a range of African Americans with various complexions, there was not one woman with short hair. You see what I mean? What are millions and millions of African American women going to think, and how are they going to feel when they see that cover? It's deep! We can't forget that self-conceptualization is directly related to self-esteem, and self-esteem is directly related to our energy levels.

Young brothers and sisters must be told early that they have to focus on using their energies and smarts to create shrewd foundations for building and taking control of their destinies. Young brothers and sisters need to be told and directed to face the reality of what is required to make a foundation for a good life. And they need to be asked straight-forwardly whether they themselves would want to be born in this complex world to unprepared, teenage parents.

Young brothers and sisters need to be told and shown straight-forwardly that it is only a sense of responsibility that makes one a man or a woman. They need to be told and shown that no other concept of adulthood will be rewarded. The sexist and degrading point of view set forth in a lot of male rap music tells me that this coming generation of young black women is going to be in serious trouble unless they develop a strong movement of resistance encompassed in a strong women's liberation and independence movement. These young women must begin to resist their own demoralization. They must resist having their lives taken as a sport.

Let me say again that there is one thing that troubles me greatly about so many African American men, and that is that they have become so very un-African in their sensibilities. They have become so duped by the very same western concept of maleness which is responsible for doing them in! They don't want to be in touch with their feelings, and in that terrible western way they invest too much of their sense of being in the belief of the absolute power of the individual self. Their sense of connectedness with a cosmic force has grown too weak and is too often non-existent. That's very unfortunate because they may not know it but they are thereby forfeiting and losing a source of strength. They don't know it, but John Wayne, who would grind his boot in their neck, who represents those who do grind their boots in black men's necks, is really the type person they are using for their hero! The force that is doing them in and is tampering with their destiny is the same one after whom they are trying to model their own being. They should check that out because they do become a source of their own devastation.

Let's not be naive about power in the positive or the negative sense. You have to develop and use all of your power currencies, all of your resources. Otherwise, you will be viewed and abused *first*, as powerless, that is as not having negotiating influence; or *second*, as valueless, that is, not having resources to offer even to your own community, and that means that when the animal instinct in human beings rather than the humanitarian instinct is dominant in the power-holding and power-conserving group, you will most likely be looked upon as disposable. And somebody will seek to give the orders and somebody will seek to carry them out. The animal aspect can lead to terrible tragedy. We all have to be aware of this operating force in history and we all have to be responsible for developing our resources in various ways in order not to fall victim to that animal aspect which arises too often in what we call the human being.

Each of us has to be a resource which can be somehow useful to shaping our destiny. Life is no joy ride, so we have to expect from each person a fare, a sense of responsibility toward something and a sense of generating a legacy of some type that can be useful.

So many of the young people who think they are Afro-centric are very mistaken. Look around and see how many are caught up in a very Western style of "either/or" mentality of thinking. They think that either I'll have what I want or I don't want anything at all. Consequently, they get tied to a sense of extreme laxity or nothingness and don't develop themselves to the extent that they can. Their morale is always low and they affect the morale and drain the resources of the people around them. And this leads to family and community devastation. Another thing is that they should not confuse the privilege and leisure of the wealthy with indolence or laziness. Such a distorted and naive view of reality will certainly lead to their undoing, eternal peonage and oppression, as well as to their annihilation.

Q: Do you have any recommended readings other than the works you've already mentioned?

A: I'm glad you asked that. Yes, I do. You know, one thing there is that really disturbs me is that a lot of African

American college students are not reading the history that took place in the 1960s and 1970s. Thus, many are beginning to make a lot of simple-minded proposals about change which are going to lead them to a tragic fate. The reason they need to know history is so that they can learn that they need to be sophisticated in their developing strategies. That's what the Brer Rabbit legacy is all about, ie., political and psychological sophistication. They need first to go way back and make sure they read DuBois's essay "Of Mr. Booker T. Washington and Others" in *The Souls of Black Folks*. They need to read books like Clayborn Carson's book on SNCC; they need to find a book called *Poor People's Movements: Why They Succeed and Why They Fail*; they need to read Vincent Harding's *The Other American Revolution*, in addition to his *There Is A River* which I mentioned above; they need to read Alice Walker's *Meridian*; they need to read Mazisi Kunene's magnificent Zulu epic called *Anthem of the Decades*; they need to read writings like June Jordan's *Civil Wars*, Taylor Branch's *Parting The Waters*, and Cedric Robinson's *Terms of Order*; they need to read the works of people like Dr. Ernest Holmes found in the metaphysical bookstores; they need to feed themselves periodically with inspirational materials now so much available on cassette tapes.

There is lots of good history too, now on video-tapes. You don't have to always buy them yourself. Ask the public library to carry them. They are eager to carry materials that people will use. Tapes like Basil Davidson's "Africa: A Voyage of Discovery" in four parts, tapes on African art and music, tapes on blacks in films and black filmmakers like

"Black Shadows on a Silver Screen, 1915-1950," tapes on African American music like those on Louis Armstrong, Scott Joplin, Duke Ellington, the one on jazz piano legends by Chick Corea, tapes on the nature and history of gospel music like "Say Amen, Somebody," tapes on African American dance like "Masters of Tap" and the Alvin Ailey Dance Theatre, tapes on many other aspects of black history like the one on the Black Panther Party from "Eyes On The Prize, Part II." It's amazing how much is available on video-tape.

There are all sorts of ways to inform and inspire yourself and your family, easy ways. There are lots of videos that can teach you a whole lot, which will stimulate you and also inspire you. Both libraries and video stores have large ordering catalogs that you can scan through. Just because a library doesn't already have something doesn't mean that they won't order it. Ask them and put your ideas in the suggestion box. Then give them time. It will generally take a library three to four months to fully process an order and get the material available to be checked out.

Just think of the time we spend looking at video-tapes which hardly do anything for us. If the books I mentioned are not on the shelves of the bookstores, they can be ordered by the bookstore or people can order them themselves by looking up the price and address of the publisher in *Books In Print* which can be found in any library or bookstore. As I said, you know, sometimes a lot of people say that they don't have time to read books. Well, you don't have to read the whole book in one night, one week, and not necessarily in one month. The best way to accomplish reading a book is *a paragraph at a time.* Anybody can do that. So there's no excuse!

Q: Is there a final or last word?

A: Yes. First, let's be careful about how we conceptualize existence. It is crucial to remember that race is not a fixed state of being but an experience of being. Sex is not a fixed state of being but an experience of being. Race is a vehicle of being, a vehicle for experience. Sex is a vehicle of being, a vehicle for experience. Until we human beings understand this, we'll never begin to comprehend the operation of the laws of karma. Until we begin to understand this, we'll never begin to understand and comprehend the laws of cosmic justice and cosmic responsibility.

And second, each person must remember that *everybody* has a worldview. Everybody! Be honest about it. Out of what or out of whose world view are you operating? Ask yourself that. Everybody has behavior characteristics and behavior patterns and attitudes. What I mean, for example, is: Do you see the mountain as a challenge or obstacle? Do you live mostly a chance-determined life (and teach or impart the same to your children!) allowing life mostly to operate upon you, or do you work through systems that will give you greater advantage to operate upon life? Are you sitting waiting for a liberator or are you participating in the liberating process? The way you answer these questions will help you to understand something about your own worldview, and more than that, about your own identity.

Your worldview determines your behavior and attitudes, so don't say you don't have a worldview because you certainly have behavior and attitudes. You can't get by nor through that! So you might as well fess up. The important thing is that we can change, we can improve our worldviews, and consequently we can change our behavior. And if you can change your behavior you can change your destiny. Bit by bit and sometimes by leaps and bounds you can! Let me end with the quotation from *Anthem of the Decades*, the very great book of Zulu wisdom: "Whoever abandons his home still travels with his pain. / Our greatness forbids us to flee from adversity. / The secret of life lies in the errors we commit; / Those who fail are also those who can rise by their courage."

Q: Thank you, Scribe, for sharing with us your thoughts and your time.

A: You're more than welcome. And thank you.

(October 27, 1990)

About the Author

Erskine Peters was born in Augusta, Georgia, where he attended public schools and graduated with a B.A. degree from Paine College. Before completing his Ph.D. degree at Princeton, he also studied at Yale University and Oberlin College. He worked for two years as College Tutor at Morristown College in Tennessee, was a full-time member of the Afro-American Studies faculty for eleven years at the University of California/Berkeley, where he received tenure in 1982, and he has also taught at UCLA. He is presently Professor of English and Black Studies at the University of Notre Dame.

Other books by Erskine Peters are *African Openings To The Tree of Life* (Regent Press), *Essay Writing: An Orientation Manual* (Regent Press), *William Faulkner: The Yoknapatawpha World And Black Being* (Folcroft/Norwood Editions) and *Lyrics of the Afro-American Spiritual* (forthcoming from Greenwood Press).